Crosscurrents/MODERN CRITIQUES

Harry T. Moore, *General Editor*

A Certain Morbidness

A View of
American Literature

Edward Stone

WITH A PREFACE BY
Harry T. Moore

SOUTHERN ILLINOIS UNIVERSITY PRESS
Carbondale and Edwardsville

FEFFER & SIMONS, INC.
London and Amsterdam

To
Oscar and Gladys Cargill—
They brightened the corner
Where we are.

Preface

One of the many things Edward Stone's book, A Certain Morbidness, does is to emphasize the complexity of American literature. He shows us once again how deep it is, and he casts into its depths some illuminations of considerable importance.

His title, taken from a phrase of Herman Melville's, indicates the direction of his book. It is above all a psychological (call it psychoanalytical) study of certain phases of our literature—a study which moves from a consideration of the non-rational to a consideration of the morbid. One particularly interesting chapter, the last one, deals with the use of Association in American literature. Mr. Stone shows how this begins with Poe's detective, Dupin, in "The Murders in the Rue Morgue." Dupin, talking to the man whom Mr. Stone amusingly notes is "the nameless predecessor of Dr. Watson," uses the technique of Association as the two men walk down a street near the Palais Royal. Mr. Stone then investigates its further use in the work of other American authors, coming down to Faulkner and Hemingway.

The main part of the book, however, concentrates on six authors, discussing one or two works from each of them. We are thus given new perspectives not only on Melville, but also on James, Stephen Crane, Frost, Faulkner, and Salinger (though I would hardly join

Mr. Stone in calling the last of these a "major" writer).

The essay on Frost has a particular interest because of its examination of the poem "Spring Pools." Mr. Stone reminds us that Lionel Trilling once referred to Frost's work as "terrifying," but he doesn't mention the uproar that this caused when Professor Trilling made the statement at a celebration for Frost, many of whose admirers became angry. They had always felt the object of their admiration to be a poet of beaming optimism. Their belief was greatly undermined after Frost's death, with the first volume of Lawrance Thompson's biography of the poet, which vindicated Lionel Trilling. Mr. Stone's careful exploration of "Spring Pools" vindicates him further.

Throughout, this book is continually rewarding to read, not merely because of what the author does in the way of his expressed intention—to investigate the irrational and the morbid—but also because of the extra dividends he often gives in the way of pointing out some fascinating parallels in the work under consideration and in some earlier story or poem or essay which indeed may have been an actual derivation. In the case of Faulkner's "A Rose for Emily," for example, Mr. Stone makes an interesting comparison to the almost forgotten "Jean-ah Poquelin," from George Washington Cable's Old Creole Days (1879). In the case of Henry James's "The Author of 'Beltraffio' " Mr. Stone discovers some interesting similarities with a Reconstruction-era novel, Mose Evans, by William Mumford Baker. And in the case of Stephen Crane's "The Blue Hotel" he points out that Crane was known to have discussed Goethe's theories on the psychology of color, which probably influenced him in the use of color motifs in "The Blue Hotel," a story Mr. Stone examines with the conscientiousness and skill which *make his book an important new contribution to our understanding of American literature.*

HARRY T. MOORE

Southern Illinois University
March 17, 1969

Contents

Introduction

The title is Herman Melville's, as are some of the contents. It came to mind during the writing of some
studies of American literature (mostly fiction) when
I realized that I was also taking notes for a history of
unreason in that literature. Since these notes resulted
not from intention, it seemed to me significant that
the works under study exhibit behavior ranging from
the conventionally irrational to the morbid. This, I
think, says more about our important authors than
about my own affinities.

The psychoanalytic criticism of literature in general
was born, Stanley Edgar Hyman noted twenty years
ago, at the same time as the present century, when
Freud's *Interpretation of Dreams* appeared. Since then
a history of American literature in this light has been
slowly and thoroughly in the writing, with Oscar
Cargill ("The Freudians" in *Intellectual America*)
and the late Frederick J. Hoffman (*Freudianism and
the Literary Mind*) as the earliest important contributors. Newton Arvin's study of Melville, John Berry-
man's of Stephen Crane, Frederick C. Crews's of
Hawthorne, Henry Murray's of Melville's *Pierre*, C. P.
Oberndorf's of Oliver Wendell Holmes, and David M.
Rein's of S. Weir Mitchell and Edgar Allan Poe indicate the varying interests of other contributors—
to add at random to the lists provided in Professor

Hyman's "Maud Bodkin and Psychological Criticism" in *The Armed Vision* and in Wellek and Warren's *Theory of Literature*. Recently in *Psychoanalysis and American Fiction* (1965), Irving Malin has collected fifteen such studies of our literature ranging from "Rip Van Winkle" to a Saul Bellow novel, and including psychoanalytic interpretations of Hawthorne and Sherwood Anderson from Simon Lesser's *Fiction and the Unconscious* (1957). My own hope in this book is to contribute to this long-range, mutual, joint-stock venture, both formally and informally. Its first and last chapters are surveys, or prolegomena. The first points out the range of American fiction of interest to the student of psychology or psychiatry; the last surveys developments in one important technique of such fiction, the free association of ideas. (Leon Edel, Melvin Friedman, and Robert Humphrey have written valuable guides to this latter aspect of literature, particularly of England and the Continent.) The two survey chapters frame and, I hope, give perspective to the intensive studies contained in Chapters 2 through 7. These examine eight separate works of American literature as literature, and whereas each of them in so doing perforce interprets some form of irrationality it does so only to the extent that the work in question requires. I have become convinced that the more that literature requires explanation in terms of science, the less it commands our admiration as art; and it is the American writer as artist—albeit as Artist of the Irrational—that is the primary concern in these pages. Thus do they differ from those of a treatise, which would have to devote its greatest attention to Melville's haunting but vexing "Bartleby" and its least to Frost's "Spring Pools," probably the most perfect work of art studied in this volume. Perhaps my path and the psychoanalyst's merge at Crane's "The Blue

Hotel," which I offer as a work of art inspired by a work of science written by an artist.

The first part of Chapter 6 appeared in briefer form as "The Progress of Southern Gothic," *The Georgia Review*, XIV (Winter 1960); and the framework of Chapter 8 was published in the *American Quarterly*, XXV (November 1953) as "The Paving Stones of Paris" (Copyright, 1953, Trustees of the University of Pennsylvania). I thank the editors of these publications for allowing me to add to them and to add them to this new company.

EDWARD STONE

Athens, Ohio
January 1969

A Certain Morbidness

1

Notes on the American
Muse as Psyche

All great literature, Dr. Frederic Wertham tells us, has been abreast of the ideas of its times: Shakespeare learned from Dr. Timothe Bright, and Goethe's *Elective Affinities* put to use the findings of chemistry.[1] It should follow, then, and it does, that the tradition would continue in the literature of this country, which Goethe wished well at its birth. American fiction was long in achieving importance, yet when by the middle of the nineteenth century America produced "a novel that belonged to literature, and to the forefront of it," as Henry James evaluated *The Scarlet Letter*, it should not surprise us that it not only anticipated the modern psychological novel but the modern psychiatric novel as well, studying as it does the pathological effects of repression and obsession. Before this there had been the short fiction of Edgar Allan Poe, our first theorist and practitioner of the workings of the morbid mind in fiction. His "Haunted Palace" is dated 1839, and "The Raven" presents that form of "despair which delights in self-torture," as Poe explained it in "The Philosophy of Composition." A historical survey would come up at least to Nelson Algren's *The Man With the Golden Arm*, whose Sophie Macjinek withdraws further and further from reality until, like Tennessee Williams' Blanche DuBois, she has to be confined in a hospital for the insane. Already in one is the narrator of Ken Kesey's *One Flew Over the Cuckoo's Nest*, which combines the mad comedy of the first novel (*Don Quixote*) and the mad loneliness of the last (*The Catcher in the Rye*). Our history would take us back to a time, only yesterday, when the insane was indiscriminately classed with the criminal and confined within the same walls (Melville's harmless Bartleby is imprisoned technically for vagrancy, not for insanity), and the criminal dismissed out of hand by no less a mind than William Hazlitt's as "A book sealed," which "no one has been able to penetrate to the inside!" [2] It would end at a time when in the flood tide of the New Science (psychology) the seals of the mind were being broken one by one and the contents seen to be inexhaustible and endlessly fascinating. When modern writers flocked to Freud's new well for nourishment and inspiration, they were reversing Freud's own course. No wonder that Freudian psychiatry had in turn the greatest influence on literature of any, deriving its findings as it did from the classic and the modern writers, from myths and dreams. [3] And the waters of that well! More than all else, dreams; the ego, the libido, and the id; the conscious and the unconscious, the subconscious and the preconscious; infantile sexuality; Oedipus complex; introversion, inversion, and extraversion; fixation; anxiety; repression; projection; sublimation; neurosis, neurasthenia, and psychosis. First, theology had postulated a principle of human behavior divinely ordained (predestination). Then biology had restated the principle in scientific terms (heredity, environment). "But now the psychologists tell us / That Infancy settles our lots," Phyllis McGinley complained in the middle of this century. [4] Actually, she was simplifying: as Jung (and Freud before him) had premised, the collective unconscious went much further back than the individual unconscious. In another exactly mid-century testament—this time a cartoon—the upper middle-class customer is explaining to the bartender that "My wife's motivational ideal has always been of a societal nature, with a tendency toward ego symbolizations on a level of exteriorized herd approval. My frame of values is more involuted and contemplative, with the emphasis on the individualized rewards of experience. As there are strong emotive elements in both orientations, some kind of conflict was naturally bound to arise—"[5] an explanation that throws light not only on the drinker's latest quarrel with his wife but on Ahab's quarrel with Starbuck. The cartoon housewife through whose apartment window construction workers can be seen pounding on steel girders and who is angrily shrieking into the telephone: ". . . N as in neurotic, O as in Oedipus, I as in id, S as in subconscious, E as in ego . . . noise!!!"[6] is spelling out what may be wrong with the narrator of Poe's "The Tell-Tale Heart" (It was his eye!); and also with both the frantic Joe Christmas of Faulkner's *Light in August* and the phlegmatic John Marcher of Henry James's "The Beast in the Jungle" (Something is Going to Happen to Them). In "The American Scholar" Emerson had pointed to a dangerous condition he had found in the seedbed of our new industrial society: "Young men of the fairest promise . . . are hindered from action by the disgust which the principles on which business is managed inspire, and turn drudges, or die of disgust—some of them suicides"—a remarkably prophetic appraisal of the times by this transcendental and esthetic philosopher, evoking as it does images not only of the Great Depression suicide of the machine-tormented Hart Crane but of the frequently noted present-day, Affluent-Society avoidance of a business career by the best of our college graduates. At the end of Emerson's century, the psychologist William James would observe a pattern of conduct of this kind much more closely:

> so many of our fellow-countrymen collapse, and have to be sent abroad to rest their nerves. . . . I suspect that [the cause of these breakdowns] lies . . . in those absurd feelings of hurry and having no time, in that breathlessness and tension, that anxiety of feature and that solicitude for results, that lack of inner harmony and ease . . . by which with us the work is so apt to be accompanied. These . . . are the last straws . . . , the final overflowers of our measure of wear and tear and fatigue.[7]

Thus would he furnish, years in advance, a gloss on the imminent mental collapse of the hero of E. B. White's "The Door" (the ground comes up ever so slightly to meet his foot).

With the dawn of the nineteenth century the sun's rays fall on the statue of the newest goddess in civilization's pantheon, installed by the French revolutionaries—the Goddess of Reason. A century later, a prominent breaker of the old seals of the mind (and perhaps forger of new ones), Carl Jung, would relegate the reason to "only one of the possible mental functions," surrounded by "the irrational, that which is not congruous with reason."[8] Today, at a time when it is recognized that one person in twelve will require psychiatric care, a modern reissue of Melville's *Pierre* is edited by a psychiatrist. And fittingly: did not Melville himself examine the villainous master-at-arms, Claggart, on a couch and submit his diagnosis? (Forty years earlier he had subjected his own mind—and ours, too—to the extended analysis of "The Whiteness of the Whale.") And by 1947 there would appear that newest kind of anthology of literature, *The*

World Within: Fiction Illuminating Neuroses of Our Time, its introduction and analyses furnished by a prominent psychiatrist.

If in the intervening years morbidity and lesser degrees of irrationality have been domesticated in the American reader's consciousness, we have the passing of time, and with it the progress of knowledge, to thank. Possibly there was something *outré* and Gothic about Poe's Roderick Usher because of his great distance from his readers in space as well as in time; whereas Faulkner's Emily Grierson is no further away than the old house across the street from which Mother was borrowing a cup of brown sugar only yesterday. The strange recluses of modern fiction did not suddenly appear; their hair became white not overnight, but over the decades. As the nineteenth century grew older, it learned more and more about itself. At its beginning, Schiller had pleaded, "Grant us only a Linnaeus for the classification of the impulses and passions of man, as in the other kingdoms of the natural world," and in Charleston, South Carolina, William Gilmore Simms, who quoted the passage, complained that although all is permitted the physician of the body,"the same privilege is not often conceded to the physician of the mind or of the morals, else numberless diseases, now seemingly incurable, had been long since brought within the healing scope of philosophical analysis." [9] Yet as early as 1840 (ten years before Hawthorne's *Scarlet Letter*), T. C. Upham would publish his *Outline of Imperfect and Disordered Mental Action.* Half a century later, when the Linnaeus of the mind actually materialized in William James, he would urge those responsible for educating the younger generation according to the latest knowledge to keep in mind that our thought processes "are not the immediate consequences of our being rational beings." [10] Nor does it seem likely that James, Freud, and their contemporaries could have arrived at their concept of human personality without the work of the German philosopher Schopenhauer, who had died midway in the century.[11]

The poets learned from them all. Particularly was this true in France, where psychiatry was born. We remember that Freud learned from Charcot; and what we read in Zola was inspired, as time passed, by the medical scientist Claude Bernard. And of the Goncourts' famous statement of 1864, with its stress on science for its realism—"At this day, when the sphere of the Novel is broadening . . . , when it is beginning to be the serious, . . . living form of literary study and social investigation, when it is becoming, by virtue of analysis and psychological research, the true History of contemporary morals" [12]—of this, it seems beyond doubt to Erich Auerbach "that here the Goncourts are thinking of the methods of experimental biology." [13] In the hands of such determined literary probers, of philosophers like these—capable, as Keats had remarked, of clipping an angel's wings or, to use Poe's phrase, of dragging Diana from her car—in such hands, what would become of that most sacred of literary subjects, the grand passion? The two treatments of the relationship between man and woman confront each other across the two halves of the nineteenth century. Could one think of the pristine Eugénie-Charles love in *Eugénie Grandet* in the same terms as those of the Thérèse-Laurent attraction in *Thérèse Raquin*, of which Zola wrote: "In these brute beasts I have attempted step by step to follow the secret activity of the passions, the pressure of instincts, the cerebral derangements following on a nervous crisis. . . . [What] I have been obliged to call their remorse is a simple organic disorder, a rebellion of

nervous systems tense to the point of breaking." [14]
The Goncourts provide their own confrontation between these two versions, their own manifesto. In
Germinie Lacerteux, they warned, the public would
find not falsity but truth; not "erotic trash" or "décol-
leté photograph of Pleasure" but "the clinical examination of love."

Even in the United States, where literature such as
this was available, depending on time and place, in
translations surreptitiously expurgated, the inquiring
writer of fiction was already assuming informally the
functions of the psychologist and psychiatrist. Hawthorne, again, it is who beckons to us. "Man's most
urgent need, he saw, was 'physicians of the soul.' Psychology became the vital task of mankind." [15] From
Poe's prose one can compile a treatise on nonrational
psychology that seems remarkably in advance of its
own, phrenology-minded, times: in "The Philosophy
of Composition," "The Imp of the Perverse," and
"The Black Cat" he submits a substantial bill to modern science. We need not dwell on the confluence of
the streams of science and fiction in the "medicated"
(psychiatric) novels of Dr. Oliver Wendell Holmes.
The spinster recluse—for a familiar literary type—has
always been there, but each generation of writers has
opened a little wider the door to her chamber. Shall
we begin with Hawthorne's Hepzibah Pyncheon? Re-
membering Randall Stewart's remarks on the parallels
between Hawthorne's time and place and Faulkner's,
we are tempted to detect a foreshadowing of Miss
Emily in Miss Hepzibah, who, "though she had her
valuable and redeeming traits, had grown to be a kind
of lunatic, by imprisoning herself so long in one place,
with no other company than a single series of ideas,
and but one affection, and one bitter sense of wrong";
but all the gloom of the house of the seven gables is

created only to be dispelled. Between Hepzibah and Emily, however, there has been a succession of New England spinsters whose conduct betrays more and more the signs of eccentricity and insulation. They stop short of Miss Emily's violence, but are the more engrossing on that account. It could have been Eugene O'Neill—to cite only the most prominent possibility—that Willa Cather had in mind when she tried to account, in "Miss Jewett," for the decline in the 1930's of the popularity of Sarah Orne Jewett's stories of the New England of half-a-century before. Your typical young man from the city, "inoculated with Freud"—

> How could he find the talk of the Maine country people anything but "dialect?" Moreover, the temper of the people . . . is incomprehensible to him. He can see what these Yankees *have not* (hence an epidemic of "suppressed desire" plays and novels), but what they *have*, their actual preferences and their fixed scale of values, are absolutely dark to him.[16]

Yet there was something in those preferences and that scale of values that a later generation, regardless of the circumstances of its origin, would no longer be able to find as whimsical or droll as their grandparents had; for it was no longer possible to ignore in them the first signs of the psychological withdrawal that would yield results more and more irrational in fiction as the years passed. We can find in Jewett's "Miss Debby's Neighbors" a nostalgic attachment to the past of the region ("those good souls who have sprung from a soil full of the true New England instincts; who were used to the old-fashioned ways, and whose minds were stored with quaint country lore and traditions") and an impassioned defense of the good old days (before "all sorts of luxuries and make-shifts o' splendor that would have made the folks I was fetched up by stare their eyes out of their heads") —we can find in this something essentially akin to William Faulkner's nostalgic backward glance in "That Evening Sun" at the bygone Monday mornings when "the quiet, dusty, shady streets" of Jefferson would be full of tall, stately Negresses like Nancy, balancing immense bundles of clothes "on their steady turbaned heads," when Miss Emily's "big, squarish frame house . . . decorated with cupolas and spires and scrolled balconies in the heavily lightsome style of the seventies" on Jefferson's best street was still white; but if the moral female monsters who are the spinsters of certain Faulkner stories are the descendants of the impeccable spinsters of Jewett's nevertheless, Miss Cather is probably right in ascribing part of the difference to Sigmund Freud. Miss Horatia Dane of "A Lost Lover" is "the last that was left in the old home of which she was so fond," and she like it is isolated from and protected against the present by "a long orderly procession of poplars, like a row of sentinels standing guard," as later Miss Emily Grierson would be guarded from the present by her family-proud father. Indeed, here preciseness and orderliness are already carried to an extreme that we find as abnormal as their authors found simply odd. (Is this not precisely the relationship between Faulkner's Miss Grierson and Dickens's Miss Havisham, on whom she may have been modeled? [17]) The pink and blue morning-glories "grew over the window, twined on strings exactly the same distance apart." Sunlight does not penetrate the old hall of Horatia's house (Emily eventually locks her front door) and in her own bedroom there are seven or eight family silhouettes (Emily's father's portrait dominates her house even after his death). Why had she never married the lost lover, the sailor? "I am an old woman now," Miss

Horatia reflects. "Things are better as they are; God knows best, and I never should have liked to be interfered with."

She is already the "New England Nun" that Mary Wilkins Freeman later created, but without the humorous touches and with a need for order that has become obsessive and that has its roots in sex. In Louisa's house, everything is in its place, and when her suitor puts her autograph album and Gift Book back on the table in reverse order, she immediately relieves her uneasiness by putting them in their proper order again. She is not unhappy to see him go, and quickly sweeps up the dust that his brief stay has left. She dreads the maleness that marriage would entail: "She had visions, so startling that she half repudiated them as indelicate, of coarse masculine belongings strewn about in endless litter; of dust and disorder arising necessarily from a coarse masculine presence in the midst of all this delicate harmony."

These were, it turns out, the very years when characterizations of females by fiction writers not to the manner of New England oddity born, but educated in cities and cultures which breed scientific inquiry, were beginning to display to the American reading public qualities just as obsessive but now just as patently morbid. After Freud's theories began to spread, abnormal psychology began to have a noticeable influence on character analysis in fiction. Frederick J. Hoffman observes that "What we speak of as the 'struggle of wills' in traditional fiction, becomes, for the 'clinical novelist,' a struggle against the forces of repression. What might have been considered an honorable submission to fate, or the beautiful expression of filial piety is explained as an infantile fixation or a 'parental complex.' . . . [T]here was a renewed interest in neurotics." [18] From the day of her appearance in 1886,

Olive Chancellor created a sense of uneasiness, to say the least, among the readers of Henry James's *The Bostonians*; yet the terminology to describe the unbalance or disorder in her personality had to wait a decade or two, when Freud and his fellow clinical psychologists could supply it. Eventually, a modern critic of this novel could characterize Olive with the preciseness of scientific authority. "Her symptoms are presented with a remarkable directness: persistent hysteria, a will to power that is inseparable from a will to prostration, an unqualified aggression toward men. . . . Her fanaticism is a function of a gnarled and impoverished psyche; her destructive will, the means by which ideology is transformed into hysteria." [19] And there was the neurotic female, power-obsessed, of *Roland Blake* (1886), by a Philadelphia novelist, S. Weir Mitchell, whose contributions to psychiatry Jung himself would cite in his *Collected Papers on Analytical Psychology*.

Certainly between the circumspect behavior of the old New England spinsters and the new there now falls, more than all else, the long shadow of Vienna. The times were ripe. To accommodate "our earnest novelist ready to sit at the feet of science and avail himself of its investigations," Dr. Joseph Collins wrote in 1923, along comes Freud: "He or his disciples can explain anything in the character and conduct line while you wait. If you want to know why a given person is what he is, or why he acts as he does, Freud can tell you." [20] Malcolm Cowley recalls that "The Freudian psychology was being discussed and O'Neill dramatized its simpler aspects in 'Diff'rent' to show the effects of the repression of life. Let the ideal of chastity repress the vital forces, he was saying, and from this fine girl you will get a filthy harridan." [21] Was it not in the light of just such doctrine that readers could begin to view the strange actions of spinsters freed at long last from repression: the spinster of James's "Europe" who finally escapes maternal domination and gets to Europe, where, at last allowed the light and warmth of that sun, she begins to act scandalously? Or the filthy harridan Joanna Burden of Faulkner's novel, the Yankee recluse of the Deep South, the "tranquil" and "impervious" fanatic who reacts to her abnormal sexual relationship with Joe Christmas by becoming fat, primarily in the face (like Emily Grierson, who sleeps with the corpse of her lover).

War, that "epidemic of madness," as Jung called it, fills the wards of peacetime hospitals and the pages of modern fiction with the walking wounded of the mind. But here again, the tradition is a long one, going back, not surprisingly, to the creator of eccentric old women, Nathaniel Hawthorne. Not a patriot but a psychologist lived in that old manse by Concord Bridge and wondered about the legend that a young native, converted suddenly into a soldier, had killed the British grenadier wounded in that skirmish of 1775: what then must have happened to this young man's mind—he a murderer in a country yet to fight a war and thus in which murder was heretofore considered a crime? In "Roger Malvin's Burial" Hawthorne did write a veritable clinical study of the consequences of guilt resulting from a man's not burying a comrade-in-arms whom he could not save. We were, then, not entirely unprepared when in our own century novelists created the pathological effects of warfare on the minds of men engaged in it. The "shell shock" of World War I fighting gave us Hemingway's "A Way You'll Never Be" and "The Big Two-Hearted River." World War II fighting in the Pacific gave us Norman Mailer's Sergeant Croft, as obsessed as the Captain Ahab on whom he is modeled.

In 1925, when Van Wyck Brooks accused the expatriated Henry James of deracination and the plots of his later stories, of malaises resulting from this, he underestimated the dimensions of the society James was living in. Had he had access to James's notebooks, in particular to James's sketch of a story about a mother who chooses to let her little boy die rather than grow up to read his author-father's wicked novels, to James's note to himself that "the general idea," notwithstanding its unpleasantness, "is full of interest and very typical of certain modern situations," Brooks would have had to reopen the question of whether morbid behavior resulting from fanatical religious principles has not always been a universal fact. The "morbid" is what the physician Dr. Oliver Wendell Holmes had found in the theology of the famous charismatic, Reverend Jonathan Edwards, long before modern readers found it in the famous cutthroat philanthropist, Captain John Brown (he was doing "The Lord's business on the Lord's day," he said of the blood-lettings he initiated on Sundays in Kansas and in Virginia). And the sensitive novelist William Dean Howells, who could recognize morbidity when he saw it (even in himself) and whose life spans both the New England poets' rapture about and the twentieth-century historian's re-examination of our most famous abolitionist, was eventually in a position to see him in both lights.[22]

Our histories related the midsummer frenzy of the Salem village girls in 1692, but we can read of the frenzy in the midsummer of the life of Everyman in the poetry of Robert Frost. We have watched a century of literary experiments with the subnormal mind, with the arrested or obsessed mentality, Wordsworth's idiot boy Johnny Foy [23] and Hawthorne's imbecilic sexagenarian Clifford Pyncheon preparing us for Faulkner's Benjy Compson; and Browning's "Porphyria's Lover," for Faulkner's Emily Grierson. During that time our fiction writers have performed feats of etiology. Our dread of the color white engaged the attention of Melville, then of Stephen Crane, and yet later of that thoroughly knowledgeable Freudian, Conrad Aiken. And our reaction to certain insects, too: why do we crush the harmless crawling spider, a William Gilmore Simms character asked, and a century later Robert Frost was still pondering the mystery of his loathing of that insect. Freud's "The Etiology of Hysteria" is dated 1896; yet at the beginning of the century Coleridge had attempted to explain the mystery of the illiterate German girl hysterically raving in ancient tongues (and had anticipated the unconscious; as had Charles Lamb, the archetypes of Jung); while midway between them the character Starbuck in Melville's *Moby-Dick* was probing the same mystery of Pip's ravings.[24] As early as 1850 a work of American fiction (*The Scarlet Letter*) would describe the stream of consciousness of a character's (Hester Prynne's) mind for possibly the first time in a way that modern readers would respect; by the 1930's, the use of this technique would characterize serious fiction. And if today no one questions the validity of ambivalence as an explanation of human conduct, the nonrational ("depth") psychology that discovered the principle owes a debt to the conclusion of Hawthorne's novel, wherein he accounts for the rapid disintegration and death of Chillingworth.

Perhaps the history of the change during the past century and more in our conception of the prevalence and importance of the irrational and the morbid in the mind of man, is summed up simply in a title from the year 1901 which to Hazlitt would have been a contradiction in terms: *The Psychopathology of Everyday Life*. For "if we have not been convinced in this century that everyone is abnormal, that the so-called neurotic condition is the general condition, we have learned nothing essential about ourselves at all." [25] The author of that 1901 book, Sigmund Freud, could not know that some ten years or more before it appeared the elderly Herman Melville was observing, in a manuscript he did not finish, that whereas "in pronounced cases" the difference between sanity and insanity is easy to distinguish, "in some supposed cases, in various degrees supposedly less pronounced, to draw the exact line of demarcation, few will undertake." [26] Yet he would have noted it. We remember that in an address given at the celebration of his seventieth birthday, "Freud refused credit for having discovered the subconscious, claiming that that credit properly belonged to the writers." [27]

2

Herman Melville

They had all been jolly good seafaring stories, and the public had liked them, particularly the earlier ones. In fact, Herman Melville predicted to Hawthorne, he would go down to posterity as a "man who lived among the cannibals"; and after his death, *Typee* would be given to babies, perhaps, "with their gingerbread." [1] Alas, this would be the final and ironic reproach: to be remembered by a type of story that he himself did not respect—a commercially successful yarn on the level of the nursery—while the metaphysical broodings of his more and more troubled mind, already beginning to intrude on his fiction, publishers of fiction for adults did not want. "What I feel most moved to write, that is banned—it will not pay. Yet, altogether, write the other way I cannot. So the product is a final hash, and all my books are botches." [2] Melville was struggling to finish *Moby-Dick* at the time, and it would soon make its appearance. Although the book would prove the most magnificent botch of all great literature, for once it is precisely the botching that engages our attention, that may easily haunt us; for never were the two "ways" of writing seen in a more striking relationship, as more meaningful not only to students of the craft of fiction but to our understanding of Melville's probings into the tragic mind.

Modern scholars have contributed much evidence of the stages of the composition of *Moby-Dick* (Leon

Howard, Charles Olson, George Stewart, and Howard Vincent, most prominently), and of the methods by which Melville appears to have attempted to cover up this evidence or reduce it to a minimum. There were two yarns to splice. Did not the *Pequod*, in putting out to sea, convert the picaresque Adventures of Ishmael on the High Road into the Tragic History of Ahab, King of Nantucket? Yet basically, whichever way Melville's story originally began, there was only one story he wanted to tell, the one "banned" since the day of Adam and Eve: the story of man's rebellion against God. This, evident in the companion Chapters 41 and 42 ("Moby Dick" and "The Whiteness of the Whale"), is the most important splice of all, for it is one in which Melville reveals the basic ideational, thematic unity of his hybrid, multimooded and multisubjected story, whatever multitude of minor inconsistencies, incongruities, and mysteries might remain to mar it. For in this major act of stage-managership we can observe Melville putting Ahab and Ishmael side by side and finding them, strange to say, one and the same mind, if not one and the same person. Only in the matter of form, we discover, is the substitution of Ahab for Ishmael significant. The two men turn out on close inspection to be far more alike in their relationship toward the universe than Ishmael's posturing as a rollicking character out of a Smollett novel or than Ahab's cadenced denunciations of God in themselves would indicate. That is why the forty-first and forty-second chapters are actually two halves of one; why the first of these, the chapter on Ahab, is about Ishmael as well; and why the second, ostensibly about Ishmael, is also about Ahab. For they are both Man affronted by and confronting "the interlinked terrors and wonders of God." (Chap. 24)

As Melville insinuates, ventures, or thunders during

the vast course of his story, this consciousness of the frightful aspects of creation is universal; it is a "primordial horror" of the blackness of one's own despair. Ahab freely gives voice to it, and the cooperation from the crew that he elicits in so doing may be the more spontaneous in that it voices their own horror.[3] Ishmael refers in passing to "that demon phantom that, some time or other, swims before all human hearts"; (Chap. 52) just as earlier he confesses his inability to explain just what it was that made the crew consent so spontaneously to Ahab's quest, "what the White Whale was to them, or how to their unconscious understandings, also, in some dim, unsuspected way, he might have seemed the gliding great demon of the seas of life." (Chap. 41) In fact, the degree to which this irrational fear, this dread of finding Nothing beyond the mysterious and beguiling phenomena of existence, infects the men aboard the *Pequod* is the measure of their importance in the story; and as with them we ascend the stairs of consciousness we descend from sanity to madness.

The dread is present even in the crew, although their despair and fury at the horrors the white whale symbolizes are apparently superficial and spasmodic. They agree at once to join Ahab in his devilish hunt, and when they finally engage the white whale, the wind that speeds them on "seemed the symbol of that unseen agency which so enslaved them to the race" (Chap. 134). But Ahab, who knows their fickle of-the-earth-earthiness, has foreseen that "when retained for any object remote and blank in the pursuit, however promissory of life and passion in the end, it is above all things requisite that temporary interests and employments should intervene and hold them healthily suspended for the final dash" (Chap. 46); accordingly, he permits them to hunt all sperm whales what-

ever. And only to a slightly lesser extent is this true of
"jolly" Stubb. By the time we get to Starbuck, we
have come to a high level of mind; but even now we
are dealing with a man whose inward steadfastness
and faith incline him to concern himself with what
Howells calls "the smiling aspects" of reality. Hearing
the "infernal orgies" of the crew's drunken revelry
(Chap. 38), he yields to a rare moment of awareness
of "the latent horror" of life; but, much as we should
expect from the pious person he has shown himself to
be, he resists this awareness "with the soft feeling of
the human" in him, exclaiming, "Stand by me, hold
me, bind me, O ye blessed influences!" In the peaceful
warmth of the Japanese fishing grounds, the soothing
scene of the calm, golden sea causes Starbuck to murmur to it, "Loveliness unfathomable, as ever lover saw
in his young bride's eye!—Tell me not of thy teeth-
tiered sharks, and thy kidnapping cannibal ways. Let
faith oust fact; let fancy oust memory; I look deep
down and do believe." (Chap. 114) To the imputation that "all of us are Ahabs," he cries, "Great God
forbid!" (Chap. 123)

But if in truth "these are the times of dreamy
quietude, when beholding the tranquil beauty and
brilliancy of the ocean's skin, one forgets the tiger
heart that pants beneath it," when one "would not
willingly remember, that this velvet paw but conceals
a remorseless fang," they are not so for Ishmael—not
for long. He, we note, is a man much more "madly
merry" and "gloomy-jolly" than the ship and crew he
applies these phrases to. His is the only consciousness that truly grasps and matches Ahab's (if it is
actually possible to separate his consciousness from
Ahab's). In stature, of course, Ahab is unique on the
Pequod, and it is a uniqueness that Ahab himself
insists on: "Ye two are the opposite poles of one

thing; Starbuck is Stubb reversed, and Stubb is Starbuck; and ye two are mankind; and Ahab stands alone among the millions of the peopled earth, nor gods nor men his neighbors!" (Chap. 133) As, indeed, Captain Peleg had told Ishmael: "Ahab's above the common; Ahab's been in colleges, as well as 'mong the cannibals." (Chap. 16) But when Peleg continues his characterization of Ahab by saying that he has "been used to deeper wonders than the waves; fixed his fiery lance in mightier, stranger foes than whales," what has his riddling metaphor told us about Ahab that Ishmael has not told us about himself at the end of the first chapter: "I am tormented with an everlasting itch for things remote. I love to sail forbidden seas, and land on barbarous coasts"?

The courses of action that Ishmael and Ahab follow in the story are as widely divergent, of course, as the views that their two natures direct them to take. But we must note the correspondences between these two complex, divided spirits, as well as the patent differences in their actions,[4] if we are to perceive what broad application Melville's story has after all. Rail against "hideous allegory" though Ishmael (Melville) may, it is in creating the two-sided nature of Ishmael-Ahab that Melville has produced—whether he intended to or not—something that approaches allegory: for in these two men he has offered his readers examples of the only two courses of action open, not to Emerson's "Man Thinking" but to Man Sensing, Man Fearing, even Man Dreading the mysterious horrors of the world, visible and invisible. The chief horror, the white whale,

> To D. H. Lawrence . . . was "the last phallic being of the white man," its blood-consciousness sought out for destruction by the thin intellect. . . . To the disciple of Jung, said Mumford, it could stand for the Unconscious

itself, which torments man, and is yet the source of all his boldest efforts. There is no lack of critical challenge in these suggestions, and in so far as they stress Melville's penetration to the primitive forces of experience, to the element of the irrational, they possess a basic relevance to the book.[5]

What Moby-Dick symbolized to Ahab, we know well from the chapter of that title; but because of Ishmael's emphasis there (and elsewhere) on Ahab's "frantic morbidness" and "monomania," we tend to forget that it is the morbid strain itself that unites the two men rather than marks their separateness.[6] Ishmael explains that to Ahab the unique malignity, inscrutability, and intelligence of the white whale incarnate the mysterious sinister quality of life, a visible personification of all evil, and afford Ahab an object on which to "burst his hot heart's shell," as though that heart were a mortar. But he points out that his own voice had been added to the crew's because "A wild, mystical, sympathetical feeling was in me; Ahab's quenchless feud seemed mine." And he devotes the entire following chapter (42) to an attempt to explain his same eagerness for the "fiery hunt," prefacing that chapter with a remark that would be uncalled for if—as we usually assume—he is merely setting the stage for the appearance of Ahab. In telling us here that "in some dim, random way, explain myself I must, else all these chapters might be naught," he seems to us to be Melville himself in the act of writing a memorandum to himself; of emphasizing to himself that he must effect this splice; of warning himself that not to do so will be most damaging to his story. And splice the Ishmael and Ahab yarns, he does, as many of the passages in "The Whiteness of the Whale" and in later chapters demonstrate.

It was the whale's whiteness, he says; and he cites examples without end of the unspeakable spiritual horrors he associates with this color, the very endlessness of his examples underscoring the ineffability of the state of mind he is trying to convey. Yet as we read on, we discover that this horror can be evoked in him by various other manifestations of God's handiwork that appear to refute Design or that other dogma of the believing—namely, God's love. In Chapter 59, Ishmael describes his disgust at the giant white squid, "an unearthly, formless, chance-like apparition of life." It will be noted that equally disturbing to Ishmael is the random meaninglessness and malice of that apparition, which the whiteness underscores but which is not limited to its color; and that times without number he reinforces this feeling with metaphors of Creation taken from the predatory beasts (shark, wolf, panther) added to other apparitions like the Dismal Swamp and the Sahara Desert shocking even when not white but simply because they dumbfound a mind inculcated with a belief in the love and meaningfulness of every part of creation.

But this is also, in large part, an analysis of Ahab. In fact, to look backward and forward from Ishmael's reminder that unless he explains his own reaction to the white whale "all these chapters might be naught" is to note how much the two men are spiritually akin.

First, we can perceive that although it is by and large the fact of Moby-Dick's existence that maddens Ahab, it is also his color. A dozen times he repeats "white" (instead of merely the whale's name, which he might do with equal pertinence, for not only is Moby-Dick the only white whale: he is the only one with a name) in his harangue in "The Quarter Deck," in his confrontation with Starbuck, and elsewhere. Apparently the whiteness accentuates the rage that

Moby-Dick's "malignity" inspires in Ahab. For to him, this whale is the great emblem of the spirit of violence and hatred of the universe. From recognition of this spirit stems his blasphemy, which he asserts or confides frequently and to any ear. He tells the dead whale's head, "Thou saw'st the locked lovers when leaping from their flaming ship; . . . true to each other, when heaven seemed false to them. . . . Oh Head! thou has seen enough to . . . make an infidel of Abraham!" (Chap. 70) In "Log and Line" he tells the crew, as he takes the crazed Pip's hand: "Lo! ye believers in Gods all goodness, and in man all ill, lo you! see the omniscient gods oblivious of suffering man; and man, though idiotic . . . , yet full of the sweet things of love and gratitude." Watching an albacore seize a flying fish in its fangs in Chapter 132, he sneers to the despair-blanched, retreating Starbuck: "Where do murderers go, man! Who's to doom, when the judge himself is dragged to the bar?" And as he calls out to God himself in "The Candles," "I own thy . . . power; but . . . will dispute [it]. . . . But . . . come in . . . love, and I will kneel and kiss thee."

It is precisely this "sharkish" or "wolfish" quality of God's universe that we can see upsetting Ishmael's faith—Ishmael, who, to judge merely from Chapter 41, has a horror only of the whale's whiteness. It is important that one of his first remarks about himself is that "I am quick to perceive a horror and could still be social with it—would they but let me," for it encompasses almost everything else he says about God's world. Indeed, his particular horror—that of whiteness—is merely a fixing of his fear on a tangible, if inexplicable, quality in that world, a revulsion at its horrors that characterizes his thoughts throughout the book.

To define Ishmael's relationship to the universe, we should turn to a passage in "The Try-Works." "The

truest of all men was the Man of Sorrows," he tells us,
"and the truest of all books is Solomon's, and Ecclesiastes is the fine hammered steel of woe. "All is
Vanity.' ALL." Now, not here, but in a letter to
Hawthorne at this time Melville went on to add that
even Solomon stopped short of the ultimate truth.
What this truth was, he leaves us to guess, but we may
find out by ourselves. Solomon's wisdom, he tells us, is
"a wisdom that is woe." If all is vain, it is because all
values of good and bad, of virtue and vice, or reward
and punishment, are human and therefore not inherent. For that reason, life mocks ambition. And since
man has no proof of a hell for punishment or of a
heaven for reward, it is not worth man's time to dread
the one or aspire to the other. What man's whole duty
is, therefore, is to love God and one's fellow man,
rejoice in the fruits of one's daily labor, and not pre-
sume to say for what purpose the inscrutable Deity
decreed it all.

This "woe" of Solomon's is truly a "steel," for it is
an armor which man may gird on to protect himself
against the "deserts and griefs beneath the moon."
(And, as we shall see, it is a steel that Ishmael joyfully
accepts.) If so, then what Solomon stopped short of
must have been the horrible possibility that the inscrutability of the Creator is not one resulting merely
from the limitations of man's perception but is inherent in creation; that at bottom this amalgam of sound
and fury really, if we but knew it, signifies nothing.
This, we suspect, is the "woe that is madness," is the
atheism of Ahab's defiance of God. But it is also—for
all that his often confessed acceptance of fate may
tend to obscure it—the secret fear that besets Ishmael
as well; and not only as it manifests itself in his
chapter on the basic Nothingness of the color white,
but throughout *Moby-Dick*.

The intensity of this skepticism varies. Occasionally it is a brooding, Housman-like melancholy, as when Ishmael tells us that "mortal man who hath more of joy than sorrow in him—that mortal man cannot be true—not true or undeveloped" (Chap. 96), or when he has Ahab reflect that "equally with every felicity, all miserable events do naturally beget their like. Yea, more than equally, . . . since both the ancestry and posterity of Grief go further than the ancestry and posterity of Joy." (Chap. 106) At other times the two men give voice to deterministic thoughts. The Ishmael who in the first chapter submits that "doubtless my going on this whaling voyage formed part of the grand programme of Providence that was drawn up a long time ago" has his counterpart in the Ahab who in almost the last chapter maintains to Starbuck that "This whole act's immutably decreed. 'Twas rehearsed by thee and me a billion years before this ocean rolled." Or fatalism. In Chapter 22 Ishmael comments that the *Pequod* "blindly plunged like fate into the lone Atlantic," just as in Chapter 37 Ahab jeers at the "great gods" as deaf and blinded. Or materialism. Ishmael early speaks of "the ungraspable phantom of life," wonders why "the Life Insurance Companies pay death-forfeitures upon immortals," and in Chapter 57 wishes that "I could mount that whale and leap the topmost skies, to see whether the fabled heavens with all their countless tents really lie encamped beyond my mortal sight!" These sentiments are echoed in the Ahab who insists to the Manxman (Chap. 125) that "The dead, blind wall butts all inquiring heads at last" and who (Chap. 127) wonders "Can it be that in some spiritual sense the coffin is, after all, but an immortality-preserver? . . . But no."

In Chapter 26, Ishmael casually notes that Starbuck's bravery is equal to "the conflict with seas, or winds, or whales, or any of the ordinary irrational horrors of the world." In Chapter 49 he speaks of the universe as "a vast practical joke," and of fate as an "unseen and unaccountable old joker." And what is Ishmael's reflection that "though in many of its aspects this visible world seems formed in love, the invisible spheres were formed in fright" (Chap. 42) but a paraphrase of Ahab's assurance to Pip that he will hold his hand fast "unless I should drag thee to worse horrors than are here"? (Chap. 125) And, did Melville not tell us, could we not guess that the Ahab before whom the white whale "swam . . . as the monomaniac incarnation of all those malicious agencies," as "That tangible malignity which has been from the beginning" (Chap. 41) and the Ishmael "horror-struck at this ante-mosaic, unsourced existence of the unspeakable terrors of the whale, which, having been before all time, must needs exist after all human ages are over" (Chap. 104) are one and the same person? What is Ahab's remark that to him, the white whale is the wall imprisoning him, that "Sometimes I think there's naught beyond" but a rephrasing of Ishmael's wonder whether "by its indefiniteness it shadows forth the heartless voids and immensities of the universe"? And finally, Ahab's memorable remark to Starbuck, "Talk not to me of blasphemy, man; I'd strike the sun if it insulted me. For could the sun do that, then could I do the other . . ." can be found in paraphrase in an obscure cetological chapter (57) in the mouth of Ishmael himself: "I myself am a savage, owning no allegiance but to the King of the Cannibals; and ready at any moment to rebel against him."

But ever so gradually the courses of these two ships diverge, the pilot's sloop returning to shore and to God's gift of human society, while the *Pequod* careens madly on and, like that of the false counselor Ulysses, carrying all hands except one over the brink to be overwhelmed by night, Ishmael's cry of loyalty to Ahab's atheistic pursuit diminishing to a faint and reproachful echo.

Both faith and brotherhood retrieve him from the brink. Incapable, at last, of persisting in his Ahab-like suspicions of the nothingness beyond the appearances of this world, Ishmael declares (Chap. 99) that "some certain significance lurks in all things, else all things are little worth, and the round world itself but an empty cipher, except to . . . fill up . . . some morass in the Milky Way." And just as in the first chapter he had confessed to his ability both to "perceive a horror, and . . . still be social with it," so in Chapter 85 he describes himself as follows: "Doubts of all things earthly, and intuitions of some things heavenly; this combination makes neither believer nor infidel, but makes a man who regards them both with equal eye." Two chapters further on: "amid the tornadoed Atlantic of my being, do I myself still forever centrally disport in mute calm; and while ponderous planets of unwaning woe revolve around me, deep down and deep inland there I still bathe me in eternal mildness of joy." Fear, despair—from these he never is or will be completely free; but of rebellion, yes. In "The Castaway" he cries out: "The intense concentration of self in the middle of such a heartless immensity, my God! who can tell it?" For, he points out almost in the same breath, in referring to the harrowing experience that has maddened Pip, "man's insanity is heaven's sense; and wandering from all mortal reason, man comes at last to that celestial thought, which, to reason, is absurd and frantic; and weal or woe, feels then uncompromised, indifferent as his God." His lasting reaction, of course, is resignation, acceptance. And the "genial" mastering the "desperado" promptings of his inner self, he clings to the warmth of God's creation—to his fellow man. This, the best advice that wise Solomon could give, Ishmael embraces, and the fruit of this philosophy redeems him. Early he had found that Queequeg caused a "melting" in him: "No more my splintered heart and maddened hand were turned against the wolfish world. This soothing savage had redeemed it." Now, in the late "A Squeeze of the Hand," he sits silently squeezing case, wanting nothing more than the cleansing and the release from the horrors that ever lie in wait at the threshold of his consciousness. "I forgot all about our horrible oath," he confides; "in that inexpressible sperm, I washed my hands and my heart of it." And feeling almost an ecstasy from the fact that his hand symbolically finds itself squeezing those of his fellows along with the lumps of sperm, he paraphrases Ecclesiastes, the "truest of all books": now, he tells us in "A Squeeze of the Hand," he has perceived that "in all cases man must eventually lower, or at least shift, his conceit of attainable felicity; not placing it anywhere in the intellect or the fancy, but in the wife, the heart, the bed, the table, the saddle, the fireside, the country," he tells us, he is "ready to squeeze case eternally." His meditation, inspired by the vast congregation of mating and nursing whales in "The Grand Armada," that "this host of vapory spouts . . . showed like the thousand cheerful chimneys of some dense metropolis, descried of a balmy autumnal morning" in fact reveals a homeliness of sentiment that we would ordinarily look for in those poets of the domestic scene, Longfellow and Whittier.

But for the morbid Ahab to abate his defiance of God or to resign himself willingly to God's gift of human brotherhood is out of the question. Not that he is not as cognizant as Ishmael of the "wonders of God" as of His terrors. Curiously indeed, the following reflection comes from him, and not from Swedenborg or Emerson: "O Nature, and O soul of man! how far beyond all utterance are your linked analogies! not the smallest atom stirs or lives on matter, but has its cunning duplicate in mind." ("The Sphynx") Nor that he does not have his "humanities," his human urgings. Visions of the peaceful life that awaits him ashore after forty years of solitary sea-life haunt him.

> "I have seen them—some summer days in the morning [in Nantucket]. About this time—yes, it is his noon nap now—the boy vivaciously wakes; sits up in bed; and his mother tells him of me, of cannibal old me; how I am abroad upon the deep, but will yet come back to dance with him."

And not only affection for wife and son but love for fellowman. He kicks Stubb with a normal anger that in itself salves the hurt; befriends the mad Pip with a touching tenderness; and at the end confesses, "Starbuck, of late, I've felt strangely moved to thee; ever since that hour we both saw—thou know'st what, in one another's eyes." And, most movingly of all, "Close! stand close to me, Starbuck; let me look into a human eye; it is better than to gaze into sea or sky; better than to gaze upon God."

But at the moment of final decision, his "fatal pride" impels him in the opposite direction from humble Ishmael, into putting aside his human inclination and insistently marching on into the mouth of God's own mortar, suffering his hot heart's shell to burst upon him and annihilate him. To this fatal pass he is led by his unswerving conviction that he is acting willy-nilly as "the Fates' lieutenant" and his deep-seated, blasphemous arrogance. In "The Mat-Maker" Ishmael had refused to concede man's utter helplessness in the blind clutch of Fate: granting Necessity ("not to be swerved from its ultimate course"); and granting Chance (which "has the last featuring blow at events"); yet neither of these rules over or is "incompatible" with freedom of the human will. The will is "free to ply her shuttle between" Necessity and Chance; in fact, even the paramount Chance is "sideways in its motions directed by free will." This, Ahab obstinately denies.

> "Is Ahab, Ahab? Is it I, God, or who, that lifts this arm? But if the great sun move not of himself; but is an errand-boy in heaven; nor one single star can revolve, but by some invisible power; how then can this one small heart beat; this one small brain think thoughts; unless God does that beating, does that thinking, does that living, and not I. By heaven, man, we are turned round and round in this world, like yonder windlass, and Fate is the hand-spike." (Chap. 132)

And Stubb has heard him mutter, "Here some one thrusts these cards into these old hands of mine; swears that I must play them, and no others." ("The Quadrant") Ishmael had pleaded with Ahab, as much as with himself, back in "Brit": "As this appalling ocean surrounds the verdant land, so in the soul of man there lies one insular Tahiti, full of peace and joy, but encompassed by all the horrors of the half known life. God keep thee! Push not off from that isle; thou can'st never return!" But his cry had gone unheeded.

The closer the final catastrophe approaches, the greater becomes the distance between the two men's acceptance and rejection of the universe. In the late chapter "The Quadrant," Ahab breaks the ship's quadrant, cursing it and "all things that cast man's eyes aloft" to God's heaven, and this in the paragraph immediately following the one in which Ishmael speaks of the fierce "unrelieved radiance" of the South Pacific sun as one of "the insufferable splendors of God's throne."

If, therefore, only Ishmael escapes, it is an ending for which Melville has been carefully preparing us. Only Ishmael in his own "dim random way" can interpret for us the plight of Ahab, of his own more daring, lost self. Appropriately, the *Rachel* rescues him, the lover of his fellowman and of "the living magnanimous earth" ("The First Lowering"); while his God-hating half fares otherwise. Sick with self, he does not, he cannot, love; and so he betrays the one characteristic common to all forms of the pathological mind. Coldly he "cared not to consort, even for five minutes with any stranger captain, except he could contribute some of that information" about the white whale that Ahab "so absorbingly sought"; he curses "that mortal inter-debtedness" that makes him, Ahab, stand by "debtor to this blockhead [carpenter] for a bone to stand on!" ("The Carpenter"); he rejects Captain Gardiner's beseeching. This is the half that is carried down to the icy depths from which Jonah had been delivered by a contrite heart—but he, Ahab, never.

No wonder, then, that Melville could confide to Hawthorne that "I have written a wicked book and feel as spotless as the lamb." Finally freeing himself from the death-grip of solitary Ahab's pity- and fear-inspiring doom, Ishmael shoots up to the surface, born again, saved by the coffin of a dear shipmate, purified and serene.

The conjunction of Chapters 41 and 42 in *Moby-Dick* and the effort that these two chapters make formally (and twenty others make in passing) to link the motives of Ahab and Ishmael for hunting the white whale are reasons for supposing that Ahab is not merely a creation apart from Ishmael but an extension of him. He differs in dramatic terms, to be sure, but intellectually he differs only in being contumacious and defiant—a difference which leads one man to choose to accept God's world and with it life and love; and the other, to spurn any dominion so inscrutable and perverse, to reject all solace and even to invite his own destruction. Now there are also reasons for supposing that yet another Melville creation, who appeared shortly after *Moby-Dick*, is in turn an extension of him. This is Bartleby the Scrivener.

I see Ishmael as a pious and reasonable man eventually brought to the state of mind of Stephen Crane's correspondent in "The Open Boat" by a growing feeling of what Faulkner calls impotence and rage: he wants to throw stones at the temple of the universe; then he comes to the appalling realization that there is no temple; yet at the last he chooses to accept the universe, substituting Man as a temple for the no-temple of God, and thereby achieves spiritual salvation. Ahab, enraged to a kind of madness by his impotence to find out whether the temple exists (and suspecting that it does not), finally confronts it, and does not survive the confrontation. The third character, Bartleby, undergoes this confrontation too. He is subjected to it rather than wills it; his is a confrontation of long duration, for all that it is told in the hasty retrospective conjecture of a paragraph and by an outsider, rather than in a head-on conflict of titans led up to in more than 130 chapters by a sensitive alter ego. Bartleby survives, but only at immense cost: learning the truth that the universe in which he is sentenced to live has no temple destroys his mind. Melville himself relates these men spiritually. Just as he bridges the distance between Ishmael and Ahab, so we can see him providing in *Moby-Dick*, even in Ahab's own words, notes for the bizarre character who would emerge only a year or two later. Adding Bartleby to Ahab, as I have added Ahab to Ishmael is, I think, to be able to grasp the degrees of Melville's fictional rebellion at the evil in the universe and the progression in the morbid effects of this rebellion on the mind of man.

Push not off from that green isle in the midst of the appalling ocean, Ishmael had warned himself and Ahab. His self had listened, and he, who told us on the first page that he was about to destroy himself before shipping on the *Pequod*, lives to tell his tale because of an object belonging to his closest friend. Nor is this the first time, he leads us to believe, that approaching madness (hypochondria) resulting from his daily commerce with man on land has caused him to go to sea. Even aboard, he slowly ventures to the mental brink again from dwelling on the thought of the mysterious whiteness that symbolizes the unfathomability of existence's riddles; again he is saved, this time both by the offered hand of human love and by the catharsis from his close-up view of the self-destroying course his alter ego Ahab is firmly holding to. Return he will, to man and shore and sanity.

Supposing, however, a fiercer man, sane in every respect except that of his unyielding pursuit of this same unfathomability, and you have a character who is rightly termed monomaniac by his creator. Like Hamlet, he is mad only north-north-west, but this is the only wind direction for this voyage in particular. For, however rationally, even shrewdly, he manages his crew, it is solely for the purpose of guaranteeing the success of the underlying purpose of the voyage, which is an insane one. He is mad, then, only in part, and in a grand way, and thus is magnificent enough to play the tragic part Melville has written for him. If he were totally mad, he would move us not to pity and fear, but to something else, possibly merely to pity, as does Don Quixote, to whom reality (the windmills) is fabulous (giants), but who harms no one; or to terror alone, as does Adolf Hitler, whose personal fable is reality, and who gives orders to burn his own windmills if he cannot have them and so orders the greatest destruction of modern times. As Melville tells us about Ahab, "all men tragically great are made so through a certain morbidness."

If we pity Bartleby, it is because he is completely and harmlessly mad. There is, as Ishmael has told us, "a wisdom that is woe; but there is a woe that is madness." Or, perhaps, when ye know the truth it shall make you not free but mad. This wisdom, this truth is that "All is vanity. . . . ALL." Or so it must have seemed, Melville guesses, to "a man by nature and misfortune prone to a pallid hopelessness" required to spend his days sorting dead letters. These are a symbol of the frustration and perversity of fate, of the vanity of the best human wishes. And to think of dead letters, as Melville asks us to, in terms of dead men is to grasp his point that no matter what effort one human makes to divine the essence of existence, it is doomed to defeat by the reckless, whimsical impudence of the workings of fate. There are no answers possible, there are only walls, and these are impenetrable. For Bartleby, the walls of "Wall Street" (an important play on words in the sub-title which Professor W. M. Gibson has reminded us of [7]) take up where his late duties in the dead-letter office leave off. By the time we meet him, he has lost his reason and is in no position to recognize the sincerity in the help that is his for the asking from his kind employer. He has collided with the "dead, impregnable, uninjurable wall," figuratively, of Moby-Dick's head (as Ahab did), that "dead blind wall that butts all inquiring heads at last."

I should like to take Professor Gibson's hint that we read "Bartleby" in the light of *Moby-Dick*. I think that we all must, for not only does the trope of the wall that Ahab refers to in connection with the white whale in his address to the crew reappear as the guiding trope of "Bartleby," but the novel has other specific foreshadowings of the short story and this strongly suggests that Melville was thinking of the central problem of the two fictions more or less interchangeably, however antipodal the settings of the two.

First, one or two details unimportant in themselves. The nickname given to one of the lawyer's two regular copyists, and suggested as "expressive" of his person or character, is "Nippers"—a word which had come in for a paragraph-long cetological definition in Chapter 94 of *Moby-Dick* ("A Squeeze of the Hand"). Here it is described as a kind of shipboard squilgee, hoe, or deck swabber made from the tendons of the tapering part of the whale's tail; whereas in the Bartleby story the word seems to express the forceps or pincers quality of the copyist's actions—his jerkiness and continual concern for mechanical adjustments on his desk. And I find no greater importance in Melville's claim in Chapter 32 of *Moby-Dick* ("Cetology") that systematizing cetological data "is a ponderous task," that "no ordinary letter-sorter in the Post-office is equal to it." There is, however, a possibility that in selecting for his example of ignominiousness of livelihood, of absence of intellectual challenge, a postal clerk's duties, Melville was venturing already toward something even more stultifying, toward the fruitless kind of letter sorting done in the part of the post office where Bartleby had worked. Nor is this the only link with the dead-letters theme, as we shall see.

My third exhibit, while even less noteworthy at first glance than the other two, is in its way a considerable one. When the lawyer comes upon Bartleby lying on the ground in the Tombs prison yard he experiences, from touching his hand, a strange sensation, "a tingling shiver ran up my arm and down my spine to my feet." He closes the dead man's eyes and to the grubman's question as to whether Bartleby is "asleep," he answers with a murmur, "With kings and counselors." That phrase was well known, of course, to Melville's generation, familiar as it was with the Book of Job; and Melville probably fondled it as he did the phraseology of the Book of Jonah (which we can find in *Billy Budd* as well as in *Moby-Dick*). Therefore the fact of its use in *Moby-Dick* is of less importance than the tone it gives to its context here. I am referring to the four-inch chapter (No. 97), "The Lamp." Ostensibly only cetology is under discussion here: specifically, the abundance of the illumination available to whaling-ship seamen's quarters in the forecastle, because of the ship's cargo, that would be an unheard-of luxury in merchantmen, whose crew members must get about their living quarters completely in the darkness. But what arouses one's wonder is the tenderness and reverence with which Melville describes the off-duty watch as they lie asleep. Coming down from the deck to the forecastle, he says, "for one single moment you would have almost thought you were standing in some illuminated shrine of canonized kings and counsellors. There they lay in their triangular oaken vaults, each mariner a chiselled muteness; a score of lamps flashing upon his hooded eyes." In the next breath, Melville has gone on to his contrast between this and the darkness of merchantmen's crews' quarters, but in the *con amore* touch of this passage there is more of interest to us than the cetology in the chapter. Kings and counsellors lying in illuminated shrines, oaken vaults, chiselled minuteness of features, hooded eyes —all this is closer to Albrecht Dürer than to the companion descriptions of the novel in which it is imbedded; moreover, the compassion and outright affection are suggestive not only of Whitman's amativeness but of the tenderness with which Melville voices the phrase from Job in "Bartleby," where the body is truly one with the great of the past, rather than, like those of the *Pequod's* crew, seeming to be. I do not know of a more moving profession of "that unshackled democratic spirit" that Melville had referred to in "Hawthorne and His Mosses" and that he invoked so thunderingly in the "Knights and Squires" chapter of *Moby-Dick:* "this august dignity, . . . that abounding dignity which, on all hands, radiates without end from God Himself!" The Andrew Jackson and the Ahab of *Moby-Dick* are thus to be linked in innate dignity with the poor scrivener of Wall Street (thus does God cull his "selectest champions from the kingly commons"). Certainly each passage gains from being read in the light of the other.

These are at best peripheral considerations. There are two other, much longer, passages, however, which deserve more attention, for they bear closely on the theme of the Bartleby story. The first of these takes up the last part of Chapter 71, which largely tells "The Jeroboam's Story." Here we listen first to the story of a dead man and then to the story of a dead letter. The first and major business of this chapter is to foreshadow Ahab's fate. The *Jeroboam's* captain gives Ahab proof of the white whale's mysterious omnipotence and uncanny malice: it has killed only the chief mate, who had "burned with ardor to encounter him"

and leaves boat and all other crewmen literally un-
touched. Add to this the part played by the crazy
Gabriel, who had predicted the chief mate's death and
now predicts Ahab's similar fate if he persists in hunting the white whale, and we can well believe, as Melville remarks in the last words of the chapter, that
"after this interlude," as the *Pequod*'s crew returned
to their work, "many strange things were hinted in
reference to this wild affair." But in the intervening
paragraphs our attention has been shifted to letters, in
particular to what turns out to be a dead letter. These,
Melville tells us, are a common occurrence on the high
seas: "Every whale-ship takes out a goodly number of
letters for various ships, whose delivery to the persons
to whom they may be addressed, depends upon the
mere chance of encountering them in the four oceans.
Thus, most letters never reach their mark; and many
are only received after attaining an age of two or three
years or more." Now it happens that the *Pequod* has a
letter for the *Jeroboam*. It is a dead letter in several
ways. It looks ghoulish (covered with green mould as
it is, after its long confinement in a dark ship's
locker): "Of such a letter, Death himself might well
have been the post-boy." It is addressed to a dead
man, the chief mate, Harry Macey. And it is refused
delivery, Gabriel insisting that Ahab deliver it to
Macey himself when Ahab is killed by the white
whale.[8]

As a whole, this chapter is almost a tour de force of
the supernatural, beginning as it does with the sudden
and magical appearance of a breeze on the becalmed
ocean, stressing the clairvoyant might of the white
whale, and closing with a prophecy aweful in its po-
tentiality. But we also see, in the section devoted to
the letter, a prominent example of the cruel frustration of fate that will madden Bartleby. For the only

letter that the *Pequod* has for the *Jeroboam* is addressed to the only man on that ship to whom its news
is meaningless—the only member of the crew who is
dead. To notice this is to be reminded at once of the
close of "Bartleby," that brooding cadenza on life's
frustrations that the employees of the dead-letter
office spend their days annotating: "Sometimes from
out the folded paper the pale clerk takes a ring—the
finger it was meant for, perhaps, moulders in the
grave; a bank-note sent in swiftest charity—he whom
it would relieve, nor eats nor hungers any more; par-
don for those who died despairing; hope for those who
died unhoping; good tidings for those who died stifled
by unrelieved calamities. On errands of life, these
letters speed to death."

What adds to our interest in this famous passage is
that the part of the Jeroboam chapter that I am discussing, when viewed in the light of "Bartleby," can
be seen as not merely an isolated anticipation of the
Bartleby theme, but a continuation and exemplifica-
tion of a philosophical musing on the perversity of our
fates in the immediately preceding chapter that, while
in terms of dead whales rather than of dead letters, is
identical in tone and its technique of antithesis or
irony to the musing on the dead-letter office that I
have just quoted from "Bartleby." In Chapter 70
("The Sphynx") it is Ahab speaking, to the head of a
whale, and citing instances of cruel and perverse fate
from ships' cruises, yet it could as easily be the narrator of the tale of "Wall Street."

> That head . . . has moved amid this world's founda-
> tions. Where unrecorded names and navies rust, and
> untold hopes and anchors rot; where in her murderous
> hold this frigate earth is ballasted with bones of mil-
> lions of the drowned. . . . Thou hast been where bell
> or diver never went; hast slept by many a sailor's side,

where sleepless mothers would give their lives to lay
them down. Thou saw'st the locked lovers when leaping from their flaming ship, heart to heart they sank
beneath the exulting wave; true to each other, when
heaven seemed false to them. Thou saw'st the murdered mate when tossed by pirates from the midnight
deck; for hours he fell into the deeper midnight of the
insatiate maw; and his murderers still sailed on un-
harmed—while swift lightnings shivered the neighbor-
ing ship that would have borne a righteous husband to
outstretched, longing arms. O head! thou has seen
enough to split the planets and make an infidel of
Abraham . . . !

What was appalling enough to split the planets or to
make an infidel of Abraham—this it is that by and
large has made an entranced madman of Bartleby.
Ahab has been storing all these instances in his hot
heart's locker to hurl them against the unfeeling God
of the universe when he finally succeeds in grappling
with him or his agent; Bartleby has been overwhelmed
by them and rendered catatonically passive, his mind
liberated from his ordeal, like little Pip's, by the mercy
of madness. "All that most maddens and torments; all
that stirs up the lees of things; . . . all that cracks the
sinews and cakes the brain; all the subtle demonisms
of life and thought; all evil, to crazy Ahab, were visibly personified, and made practically assailable in
Moby Dick." (Chap. 41) To the meek middle-class
wager-earner of New York City, all these were visibly
personified, if by no means assailable, in the thousands of dead letters Bartleby had had to process.

Even the narrator of "Bartleby," an average American of the mid-nineteenth century, senses from the
overthrow of this insignificant clerk's mind that there
are more things in the inner life of a wage slave in a
large city than are dreamed of in his own philosophy.

Professor Gibson is quite right in suggesting that "the vehicle" of the Bartleby story "may not be adequate to the thought"; yet for all its inadequacy the vehicle's mind does reach at least the vestibule of the allegorical significance of Bartleby's fate. At least so I interpret the *nunc dimittis* the lawyer pronounces for his old employee: "Ah Bartleby! Ah humanity!" And in his brief admission that when he considers what may have driven Bartleby mad, "I cannot adequately express the emotions which seize me," is not the extraverted lawyer-narrator in essence echoing what the introverted sailor-narrator of *Moby-Dick* had said when attempting to set forth the true dimensions of the alarm wakened in his soul by his consideration of the whiteness of the whale? How, Ishmael had asked, "can I hope to explain myself here"; and "so mystical and well-nigh ineffable was it, that I almost despair of putting it in a comprehensible form."

Yet, setting their observations alongside the fates of the two men for whom they serve as chorus, we find that Melville does put his message into comprehensible form after all. It is simply that man may not plumb the depths of the world's mind without paying the price of death, whether of the body or the mind: the "madness of vital truth" of Lear, as Melville had phrased it only the year before *Moby-Dick* in "Hawthorne and His Mosses." Ishmael had heeded the warning given to Adam by the archangel in Milton's poem; Ahab, like Ulysses and Prometheus and Faust before him, had brooked no restrictions on his intellectual pride and had been buried alive; Bartleby, opposing no one or thing that we know of, is one of the unburied dead. He has learned over the years in the middle of New York City what Pip learned immediately in the middle of the ocean: that heaven's sense is man's insanity, "and wandering from all mortal reason, man comes at last to that celestial thought, which, to reason, is absurd and frantic; and weal or woe, feels then uncompromised, indifferent as his God." With justice so savagely dispensed in this world, who's to respect the Judge? If the race does not go to the swift, one is free at last to loiter. If the law courts can sentence to death for killing his mother a man formally charged with killing a stranger, is there not an absurdity, an indifference in our universe benign enough to embrace? With which Ishmael, Ahab, and Bartleby join hands, and in the circle which this shock of recognition runs around they link hands with the Preacher and Albert Camus.

3

Henry James

He might, Henry James told himself, put to literary
use Edmund Gosse's story of the sad life of John
Addington Symonds, particularly of the rift between
the author and his wife, a woman "in no sort of
sympathy with what he wrote; disapproving of its
tone, thinking his books immoral, pagan, hyperaes-
thetic, etc. 'I have never read any of John's works. I
think them most *undesirable*.' " Couldn't this be a
story of war between "the narrow, cold, Calvinistic
wife, a rigid moralist; and the husband, impregnated
. . . with . . . the love of beauty . . . and aggravated,
made extravagant and perverse, by the sense of his
wife's disapproval"? The victim would be their child,
"who either bolts, as he begins to grow up, and becomes a lout and ignoramus, equally removed from
both [parental] tendencies—leading a stupid and vegetative life; or else, more pathetically, while he is still a
boy, dies, a victim to the . . . heavy pressure of his
parents. . . . If it were not too gruesome, the mother
might be supposed to sacrifice him rather than let him
fall under the influence of the father." Thus, Henry
James to himself in the London spring of 1884. Understandably, he warned himself that the writing of
such a story "would require prodigious delicacy of
touch; and even then is very probably too gruesome—
the catastrophe too unnatural."

Yet, try it he would and did, "The Author of
'Beltraffio' " in fact appearing in print only a few

months after his notebook entry. After all, he assured himself, "the general idea is full of interest and very typical of certain modern situations." [1] Which in turn leads us today to wonder: was James merely trying to justify his story, or could he have had another such situation in mind? If not "very typical," was the situation in "The Author of 'Beltraffio' " not unprecedented in the fiction of the time?

Let us move westward in space four thousand miles, to rural Mississippi, and backward in time ten years, to the Reconstruction era. The narrator of our deeply-buried novel by a man named Baker is a young lawyer from Charleston named Anderson. He is learning what he can about the region and its strange people, none stranger than Mrs. Evans, Mose's mother. A knowing native describes her,

> "Vixen. Virago. Termagant. Xantippe. Should have been ducked to death as a notorious scold years ago. . . . She killed her husband. . . . He was a professor in some Georgia college, years ago. Like those dry old pedants, fell desperately in love with his wife when a blooming girl, because, I suppose, she was so pretty and so ignorant. Mold her, you observe. Very soon she broke him up in Georgia. They had to move and move . . . until they wound up here, where he died. Sir, that poor fellow was scientifically scolded to death! . . . I knew him. . . . He had been driven into a kind of dazed insanity long before he died. His poor body held out longest, being only the secondary object of her assault. The son does not know how to read, sir!" [2]

But the son in question is a grown man! Since Odd Archer, the informant, is a most unreliable source of information, Anderson, the narrator-stranger, makes allowances. Yet, he tells us, "Brown County agreed that the woman had worried and scolded the miserable husband to death. Somehow she had embroiled

and broken him up along a series of downward re-
movals. What books remained to him were his only
refuge. . . . I would like greatly to know whether they
were sold for bread, lost in their many moves, burned
accidentally. . . . I do not certainly know . . .
whether or no Mrs. Evans in her storms of temper did
really, as Brown County asserted, rend to fragments
and burn the poor fellow's volumes to the very last
leaf . . . [but] I think this quite likely." (56–57)
Anderson's first personal experience with Mrs. Evans
inclines him to believe everything he has heard about
her. Later he speculates aloud to his companion, General Throop, asking why Mose's mother "has allowed
him to grow up untaught. Jealous even of books, because she never opens one? Hating them as the preference of her husband, his last resort from her? Or sheer
indifference and brutal ignorance!" (59)

The son so strangely victimized gives his name to
the title of this book, and the subtitle gives its warning of the incredible situation that the book will offer:
"A Simple Statement of the Singular Facts of His
Case." Understandably, objection was raised at once
to their singularity: one reviewer confessed his inability to believe "that any woman should entertain such
a jealousy of her husband's books as to bring her son
up in an ignorance so great that he knows not even
how to read." [3]

Some time before Anderson left Charleston, he and
his bride had wondered about coming events. The
strangest part of all, she had told him with clouded
eyes, lay in the future. " 'How do you know, Miss
Medea?' I ask. 'Wait, O Jason, and you will see!' she
replies." As an unconscious appraisal of the family
situation her young husband will be told about when
he gets to the civilization of Mississippi, it is practically clairvoyant; only in Euripidean terms can so

outrageous a plot be imagined. This is also true of
Henry James's "The Author of 'Beltraffio.'" As Leon
Edel has said, the fact of its main figure being a writer
"is incidental to the central drama. It is in reality a
Medea-tale, of a female figure who sacrifices innocence to her own cruel destructive vision." [4] In James's
tale, to be sure, the victim, like Medea's, is a child, the
son of the novelist; in Baker's novel, it is more scholar-
husband than son (who eventually rehabilitates himself). And there are other differences. Yet the fact
that the two mothers are so atypical of female characterization in American fiction of the times in the same
pathological way makes it worth our while to speculate briefly as to whether Henry James got his *donnée*
here, as well as from Edmund Gosse. [5]

Mose Evans was written by a minister named William Mumford Baker (1825–83). It is a lively, sentimental, and occasionally droll novel that opens in
Charleston but travels to and comes to rest in Mississippi. Its color, localized thus west of Harris, east of
Harte, north of Cable, and south of Eggleston, par-
takes of that of all these writers, but not of their
magic. It is primarily a story of love, and as such, not a
remarkable one. Who will Agnes marry—Agnes, the
only, beautiful, cultured daughter of the ruined
Charleston grandee, General Throop? Will it be the
lawyer Clammeigh (his name, a program note)? Or
the minister Parkinson? Or possibly the ghost of her
beloved brother Theodore, killed in battle? None of
these, we guess too early; rather, that least likely, that
most smitten and tireless of suitors, Mose Evans,
handsome son of nature, mighty with clenched fist
and hunting rifle. (A close resemblance to him appears in the first of the two outcomes James projected

in his *Notebooks*, as quoted earlier: "a lout and ignoramus, equally removed from both [parental] tendencies—leading a stupid and vegetative life.") Baker's
novel relies, then, chiefly on the suspense of romance.
It proceeds from our early rejection of such a marriage to our final acceptance (after Mose has educated
himself by reading, college, and travel). To set his
scene, then, Baker had to provide for the initial utter
unsuitability of the young man to Agnes; this he did
with Mose's illiteracy. For this reason, and for it
only, does Baker introduce the termagant mother.
And shortly afterwards—no longer, in fact, than necessary for us to meet this woman in person—he kills
her off. (Though this may be necessary to the development of the love plot, like the untimely destruction of
Mercutio, unfortunately, it removes a character in-
herently more interesting than the hero of the title.)

Now, the author of *Mose Evans* had had his narrator reflect parenthetically that "there is ever a Beatrice
. . . for sufferer as for poet." (134) And James's poet,
Mark Ambient, the author of *Beltraffio*, is—in a stroke
of irony worth a second's thought—married to a
woman of just this name. There are basic similarities,
moreover, between Mrs. Ambient and Mrs. Evans.
Chief among them is the incongruity between their
outer and inner selves, their physical attractiveness
and their latent bigotry. When he first meets Mrs.
Evans, the narrator, already knowing a great deal
about her, is in a position to penetrate appearances.
She strikes him as "simply a tall, well-looking, neatly
dressed female who had worried her husband to death,
and who might . . . drive us from under her roof any
moment by her termagant tongue." (52) As we shall
see, he learns quickly that hers is basically a Funda-
mentalist disapproval of books, her mind keeping itself as unsullied by them as her hands keep her house

spotless. James's young American narrator, knowing nothing about Beatrice Ambient, is favorably impressed on their first meeting: she was "slim and fair, with a long neck and pretty eyes and an air of great refinement. She was a little cold, and just a little shy," he notes, "but she was very sweet, and she had a certain look of race, justified by my afterwards learning that she was 'connected' with two or three great families." He concludes that "Mrs. Ambient, delicate and quiet, in a white dress, with her beautiful child by her side, was worthy of the author of . . . *Beltraffio*." And Ambient later tells him that when he married her, ten years before, he had thought her not only beautiful, but an angel. But the narrator by then is suspicious enough to reflect that Ambient had neglected to ask himself just what Beatrice was an angel of; and when he completes his understanding of her, the characterization that emerges is as sinister as Baker's, and for the same reason. Though no termagant, Beatrice rejects all around her, except her son, with varying degrees of intensity. She considers her husband's books, which she has not read, "most objectionable"; she hates his sister; and she betrays her dislike of the narrator, who finally grasps the capability of this woman for evil: "I am obliged to say that the signs of a fanatical temperament were not more striking in my hostess than before; it was only after a while that her air of incorruptible conformity, her tapering, monosyllabic correctness, began to appear to be themselves a cold, thin flame. . . . [If] she had a passion at all, it would be that of Philistinism." He observes that she is receiving a call from the vicar's wife when he meets her. Eventually Miss Ambient tells him that Beatrice's opposition to Mark's writing "comes from Beatrice's being so religious, and so tremendously moral, and all that."

Now, in equally important ways, the two authors are far apart. Granted that each woman's revenge on a husband results in mistreatment of a child: Baker's Medea has killed her husband before the curtain rises, whereas James's acts demonically at the dramatic close of his play. And no parading of similarities can disregard the widely different moods that pervade the two stories as a result. Whereas Mrs. Evans simply sets the stage for a love story, Mrs. Ambient dominates the stage of a tale of hate. And whereas a henpecked husband (even one pecked to death) may inspire in us a pity inevitably mixed with amusement, a child in effect murdered by his mother can inspire nothing less than horror.

Before Baker removes Mrs. Evans, however, he produces an effect or two that may have lingered in James's memory long enough to produce their echoes in his own story ten years later. One is of the militant possessiveness of the woman, revealed early in the story. Anderson and General Throop, her distinguished new neighbor, have come to call on Mrs. Evans. The general has merely mentioned that he has no sons, but that he has a daughter. Then, moved by grief at the memory of his dead son from contemplating Mrs. Baker's own handsome and virile son Mose, he praises Mose to her and concludes that she must be very proud of him. Her reply is surprising and sudden: " 'He is all I have!' . . . and she was halted, I saw, at the mention of that daughter!—with reference to any possible results concerning her son, halted, like a female panther guarding her cub." At last Anderson sees: "And I began to understand this Xantippe, by help of what I had heard, through and through! . . . 'You seem to be pleased at something, sir?' It was the panther again, with her head ever so little upon one side, a gleam of danger in her eyes, and quicker knit-

ting!" (54–55) Did any of this characterization contribute to the making of the Beatrice Ambient who
"has got the boy" (Mark tells his visitor with a double
meaning apparent at once); who refuses to let Dol-
cino come to his father, even in the presence of a
stranger; and who eventually locks her husband out of
the sick child's room?

The other is a commendable attempt by the narrator of this unfortunate contretemps to remedy it with
a suggestion that goes wrong. Sensing trouble in that
last question of Mrs. Evans's, young Anderson finds a
reason for leading the General off the panther's premises by reminding him that Mrs. Evans is probably a
busy woman; but he follows this with: " 'Were you
[General] to seclude yourself from all the outer world,
as you threaten, you would have to take to books as
some persons take to drinking!' And, to make my
blunder worse, I glanced around as I said it. 'Not one!
Except an old Bible, not one book or paper in the
house!' Mrs. Evans said it out, and I to myself in the
same instant. I began to take deeper interest in her!"
(54–55) She, in turn, once led to this distasteful
topic, begins to give General Throop her version of
the history of her marriage, but not—the narrator
quickly adds—"Not at once. Doubtless she brooded
day and night over her story, and it forced its way out
by a sort of fermentation during our after acquaintance." (55–56) This blunder, of course, does not effect
any further action in the novel. But the blunder made
by James's narrator, equally desirous of reconciling
antipathies, has disastrous results. When Mrs. Ambient consents to his proposal that she read her husband's work (made in hopes that acquaintance with it
will remove her objections), it is the very reading, at
long last, of her husband's fiction that prompts her to
bring on their son's death, thus betrays her madness.

The brief scene in the Evans house—a defeated patrician of the Old South paying a call on a shrewish housewife of a region new and raw, as related by a quick, observant young Charlestonian of Yankee stock —is over soon after it begins. But if it impresses the reader today, as almost no other scene in *Mose Evans* is capable of doing, this may be because it is a Jamesian scene. In fact, it is just possible that from so unlikely a source arose that complicated story of relationships that is "The Author of 'Beltraffio.'" For, center of interest though Beatrice Ambient is, how is it possible to think of James's story without taking into account the ramification of personal relationships, all of which contribute their share to the accomplishment of James's theme: the gradual tearing away from the narrator's eyes of the veils that mask Beatrice Ambient's madness. Mark, the esthete, and Beatrice, the bigot; Beatrice and Mark's sister, the attitudinizing Miss Ambient; Beatrice and the narrator, the impressionable and hopeful young American; and the narrator and Mark Ambient himself—here again, Baker's story may have served as a point of departure for James's.[6]

In any event, to our point here is not whether James borrowed from art or sketched from life, but what he did with what he borrowed, and why. Perhaps he remembered (even unconsciously, it may be) Baker's characterization of a pretty but fiercely possessive woman whose insane hatred for books on religious grounds warred with her husband's bookish nature and eventually killed him and enslaved her son's mind, as she appeared in a run-of-the-mine love story of ten years before; remembered her and redesigned her into the center of interest of his own story, prompted by Gosse's recent conversation. Composed, that is, from this drawing, a study in depth of four people. And from Baker's narrator-intruder's helpfully intended but meddling remark, brought about an ironic result "probably too gruesome," "a catastrophe too unnatural" for the mind of his generation to accept.

And yet perhaps if the catastrophe is no longer too unnatural for us to accept, James is as deserving of credit for the broadening of our understanding of morbid behavior as the psychologists formally working in this field in his day. The labyrinthine ways of the female character—that "dark and vicious place," etymology reminds us, in which the very word hysteria was born—had been familiar territory to the Greek dramatists. Euripides' Medea had murdered her children as revenge on her husband. Sophocles, successful with natures "poisoned by narrow fanatical hatreds," with his "special insight into morbid psychology," had created an Antigone who had killed herself because of her obsessive love for her brother. But the Victorian scholar Jebb, who removed the evidence of this from Sophocles' text,[7] was no more capable of accepting as genuine so morbid an extreme of female conduct than had been the *Harper's* reviewer of Baker's book in 1874. The area was one into which American authors had not ventured far, if at all, in James's time, but it would never again be safe from novelistic intrusion. James himself had ventured into it before and would venture into it again in creating the Olive Chancellor of *The Bostonians,* the Adela Chart of "The Marriages," and the governess of "The Turn of the Screw." Eventually, William Faulkner, abashed by no such consideration for his readers' feelings as James was incapable of escaping,[8] would uncover the morbid mind of male and female alike with the casualness of the operator of an X-ray machine.

4

Stephen Crane

Judge a writer not merely on his successes but his failures: these do much to indicate his scope, said Melville (about Hawthorne) and said Faulkner (about Wolfe). In *The Red Badge of Courage*, Stephen Crane had written so convincingly about the reactions of a normal young recruit to the horrors of war that war veterans congratulated him, who had been born six years after the surrender at Appomattox Court House. No such acceptance awaited Crane's frequently reprinted story, "The Blue Hotel," which was twice rejected by editors and whose imperfection as a work of art not all the dogged devotion of Crane's admirers has been able to do more than qualify. Here Crane opened with and maintained at considerable length a strangely compelling mood of impending violent calamity only to repudiate that effect in a final, appendage-like, section that nullifies the very effect he seems to have written the story to convey. It is possible to chart the course of this artistic failure by the degree to which Crane succeeds in integrating exterior effect of nature and human character into the main concern of his story. This, it happens, is a fascinating one, for it is nothing less than a study in hysteria, in the state of mind of a morbidly fearful city-dweller from the east as he proceeds to what seems a self-arranged rendezvous with death on a blizzard-swept Nebraska prairie. More than that, it is the first attempt made in our literature that I know of to interpret morbid human behavior from the point of view of the psychology of color. It failed, I think, but was a gallant failure and worth our examining closely.

For eight of the story's nine sections what we are faced with is a case of homicide, actually suicide, brought on, Walter Sutton thinks, by a "primitive and obscure fear . . . not comprehended by either himself or the Nebraskans . . . and . . . not adequately explained by the correspondent's assertion that he has been reading too much Wild West fiction." [1] It is, in fact, a fear that, whatever its origins in hearsay knowledge of the violence of the West, is weirdly exaggerated and heightened by the look of the West as the Swede finally experiences it in person. Specifically, it is its color, not Johnny Scully, that is his adversary, and eventually it (not the gambler) is his murderer. So pervasive is its presence that it may be thought of as a very real force capable of crazing his mind; and had Crane stuck to his purpose and stopped when he had done, "The Blue Hotel" would have achieved a forever haunting quality that we ordinarily associate with Ambrose Bierce's work.

Like *The Red Badge*, "The Blue Hotel" is a story not so much seen in color as thought in color. Late in the story, for example, the color yellow appears briefly, as we shall see. And here and there Crane finds himself turning to red. This is, predictably almost, a metaphor for bloodshed and death. In section 3, as the frightened Swede faces Scully the "murderer" in the bedroom we read that upon his "deathly pale cheeks were two spots brightly crimson and sharply edged, as if they had been carefully painted." In section 6, in the darkness of oncoming evening, the Swede fighting is reduced to the impressionistic blur of a face that occasionally shines out "ghastly and marked with pink spots." Perhaps these vivid red circles against their background of white cause the Swede involuntarily to declare his position (fearfulness) in the same fashion as, in the opening sentence of the story, Crane has had the hotel declare its own (fear-inspiring?) position. And in section 8—the last, properly speaking, in the story—as the Swede enters the saloon where he will meet a bloody death, the snowflakes are flying around a red object. An intriguing color symbolism, and one consistently used.

But first and foremost the color of this story is that rare one announced in its title. Although its use strikes one as unfamiliar (Poe being the only exception who comes to mind), Crane used it freely in his work. Attention to its use here has been called by Professor Stallman, who reminds us of Crane's "extraordinary predilection for blue, which Hamlin Garland took to be the sign manual of the Impressionists." [2] But for an awareness of the level to which Crane must have intended to raise the color blue in "The Blue Hotel," we must turn to the recollection of Crane's friend Frank Noxon that Crane was consciously working out a theory of Goethe's on the psychology of color: "He told me that a passage in Goethe analyzed the effect which the several colors have upon the human mind. Upon Crane this had made a profound impression and he had utilized the idea to produce his effects." [3] The work referred to, surely the *Zur Farbenlehre*, or *Theory of Color*, had been translated into English in 1840 (and the painter Turner had annotated the margins of his own copy voluminously, according to Professor Heinrich Henel). Certainly some of the reactions toward blue with which Crane invests the composite character of The Stranger (he is alternately the Swede, Mr. Blanc, or Crane himself) seem echoes of Goethe.

Crane had, Thomas Beer tells us, "changed trains

once at a dreary junction where was a hotel of a dreadful blue that fascinated him. His thirst for blues ran to shades of cold electric tones and this blue was a lugubrious, fainter tinge. In a hotel painted so loathesomely, some dire action must take place and, after four years, he made it seem so." [4]

If the last page of "The Blue Hotel" might be out of Tolstoy, to turn to the first page is to wonder whether one has not stumbled into Poe. We first see the hotel through Crane's eyes as a blue, screaming gesture against an annihilating white expanse. Reactions to this violent contrast are threefold, and had Crane held his Goethe in his left hand as he wrote, he could not have more painstakingly been demonstrating the latter's "general theory": "general impressions produced by single colours cannot be changed . . . and must produce definite, specific states in the living organ. They likewise produce a corresponding influence on the mind. Experience teaches us that particular colours excite particular states of feeling." The first state of mind produced by the blue hotel is on the minds of wealthy travelers from the East whose taste has been formed on gentler color combinations [5] and who need not suffer esthetic outrage such as the blue hotel offers any longer than it takes their train to fly past Fort Romper. Their reaction is one of laughter, compounded of "shame, pity, horror." On the other hand, the wild color contrast has no such significance to the second group, "citizens of this prairie town [the Scullys] and to the people who would naturally stop there [the cowboy]." These people are even proud of the color, as uncultured people are often impressed by garishness. But the Swede, who does not belong to the first group, does not belong to the other either: seemingly, he belongs in a group by himself. We must keep this in mind, even if we never find out why he was on the train to begin with. He is The Captive Stranger, and the moment he alights, his awareness is of a frightening color. It is a screaming blue. This is the color that, with red-blue and blue-red, Goethe had defined as "on the minus side"—a color which produces "a restless, susceptible, anxious impression."

This is the color of the chamber in Edgar Allan Poe's "Masque of the Red Death" in which the sinister intruder Death makes his appearance at midnight, his "mad assumptions" inspiring the entire gathering with "a certain nameless awe"; the color of the Evil Eye that crazes the narrator in "The Tell-Tale Heart." It is also the color in Crane's "The Monster" that, impinging on the consciousness of the elated Alek Williams, depresses his spirits as dusk falls.[6] In "The Blue Hotel" it is more than this; more, for that matter, than the sun in *The Red Badge*.[7] In that story the sun had been a collateral artistic symbol, whereas in our story about the morbid Swede it is nothing less than a major character—the Swede's antagonist, in fact.

When we first see the Swede he is "shaky and quick-eyed," his demoralization manifestly beginning. Into the basin Scully provides at the hotel he dips his fingers "gingerly and with trepidation," and while waiting for dinner he resembles "a badly frightened man." At dinner he indirectly announces his fear with a laugh. When, after dinner, the snow reaches blizzard intensity, he is the only one in the hotel to whom Scully's announcement to this effect is in any way upsetting, and it is possible to account for his strange behavior at this point ("The Swede remained near the window, aloof, but with a countenance that showed signs of an inexplicable excitement") by calling to mind that the view from the window is of a complete whiteness. Exactly what sort of reaction this color is capable of producing, Crane knew from Goethe: "As a hue it is powerful, but it is on the negative side, and in its highest purity is, as it were, a stimulating negation. Its appearance, then, is a kind of contradiction between excitement and repose."

So, the effect on Crane, who presents this ominous view of the "turmoiling sea of snow" for the Swede's gaze: "The huge arms of the wind were making attempts . . . to embrace the flakes as they sped. A gate-post like a still man with a blanched face stood aghast amid the profligate fury." (The third Easterner, Mr. Blanc, as yet psychologically uninvolved, is contentedly watching the card game.) Shortly afterwards, as the Swede provokes the others to annoyance and alarm with his insinuations about foul play, Crane reminds us a second time of the terror outside. Darkness is falling and the gradual changing of the whiteness to a darker color adds to the sense of ominousness. Of a large city street in winter Crane was writing in the same year ("The Men in the Storm") that "the little snow plains in the street began to assume a leaden hue from the shadows of evening." He presents the same effect here on the western plains at the moment when the Swede has announced that he will be killed in the blue hotel: "through the windows could be seen the snow turning blue in the shadow of dusk. The wind tore at the house, and some loose thing beat regularly against the clapboards like a spirit tapping." After this the whiskey feeds the Swede's fear; he dominates supper table and then card table with his bluster. Only Scully's departure to meet the evening train and his return disturb the Swede now, and each time the intrusion of a gust of wind whirling into the room evokes a curse from the Swede, otherwise engrossed in the game of cards.

When all go outside for the fist fight, we sense that

it is not only because of the greater room afforded
there but because Crane wishes to recall the reader's
attention to the force of the screaming blue whiteness
which first aggravated the Swede's original fear and set
the barometer of his morale to falling. And frightening it is (presumably to Crane, but probably to all
three Easterners, as we shall see): "No snow was
falling, but great whirls and clouds of flakes, swept up
from the ground by the frantic winds, were streaming
southward with the speed of bullets. The covered land
was blue with the sheen of an unearthly satin, and
there was no other hue save where, at the low, black
railway station—which seemed incredibly distant—one
light gleamed like a tiny jewel." This is not prose to
be read, but to be seen, and makes the reader crave,
almost demand, of Crane a visualization of the impression registered on his mind by such a sight.[8] Ten
years after Crane's death the midwestern artist George
Bellows would satisfy this demand with his painting
"Blue Snow." Here is the "unearthly sheen" of
Crane's story at last on canvas: the shadows cast by
the building on the snow in what appears to be a
suburban park create a bluish world in which the sun
and health never shine.

With section 6 the fight begins and there are two
changes in Crane's technique. First, the point of view,
already bifocal (the Swede and the author) expands
even more, so that essentially the entire section—a
long and climactic fight episode—is seen through the
eyes, now, of the Easterner Blanc. This is curious, and
a little ominous, as though in transferring the center
of consciousness Crane is showing the first sign of
losing the control of his theme, as well as preparing us
for the final shift in point of view in the final section.
Even while dressing to go outside he is so nervous that
he can hardly get his coat on. (Surely not merely at

the thought of bloodshed, for the cowboy is equally nervous.) Once he is outside, Blanc's teeth chatter, and the tenseness of the two men poised to fight "was accentuated by the long, mellow cry of the blizzard, as it sped the tumbling and wailing flakes into the black abyss of the south." Although his finer senses are revolted by the brutality of the fight, which seems endless to him, and although it is to him that Crane grants the detached and moving appreciation of the Swede's "splendor of isolation," as soon as the fight ends we learn that it is the weather itself that has become paramount in his consciousness. The wind pierces his body; the intensity of the cold suddenly becomes a menace, "and he wondered that he had not perished" (a wonder that will reappear soon in the consciousness of the third Easterner, the omniscient Crane). "He felt indifferent to the condition of the vanquished man." In fact, he, the only completely reserved person in the story up to the beginning of the fight, is the only one who is nervous now. Losing control of his feelings, he rushes inside to the hot stove and almost dares to "embrace" it.

The other change is in metaphor. In the passages just quoted, the visual blue awfulness which until now has symbolized the power of the blizzard has unobtrusively yielded to the other, nonvisual sense impressions of the blizzard's power: momentum (touch) and wail (sound). This is understandable; inasmuch as night has come on as the fight ends, the blueness of the blizzard can no longer serve as the demoralizing, the terrifying, agent. Now it is the feel and the sound of the furious winter's rages that, after the brief comic interlude of section 7, the Swede experiences as he sallies forth from the hotel. Crane's blue hotel is no longer visible; the blue snow's part in the story is now over.

Unfortunately, but inevitably, so too in a little while will be the Swede's life. As he now plunges with finality into the storm, he is at last impervious to its menace: his bruised face "felt more pleasure than pain in the wind and the driving snow." He likes this violent weather now. Certain at last that he is going to die, he has lost his fear and nervousness, which uncertainty had bred: truly anything is to be preferred to that, even death. He has sensed since morning that he may die here; it is now night, and he will end the suspense by inviting death. If, then, as we learn in the sequel section, the sentence awarded the gambler who stabs him is a light one, it is also a just one; for he and his fellow cardplayers have had no more interest in—so far from hostility toward—the Swede than did those other players in Scully's blue hotel. It was, by the time of his death, not a question of whether the Swede would be killed but who would do it and when. His first crazed premonition that "there have been a good many men killed in this room" misses its mark by only a few hundred yards. It must be borne out if he is not to undergo a complete mental collapse. His calm in the raging storm en route to the saloon and his offensive gestures inside it are tokens, as well as of the force of the great quantities of liquor he has consumed, of his acceptance of the disaster that he now knows awaits him—even of willing acceptance, as Mr. Stallman believes. And it is Crane's success in making this death seem inevitable and necessary that gives "The Blue Hotel" its amazing force, its greatness.

We have seen that the case for the foregoing interpretation rests on the solid foundation of the greater part of the first eight sections of the story. In view of this, we must find the ninth and final section a sharp departure from—even nullification of—all the effort Crane has expended to achieve his purpose. What we are asked to listen to now is a philosophical disquisition, a revelation completely foreign to the one with which "The Blue Hotel" began and which seems as surprising to us as it did to the cowboy. Johnnie's cheating cannot be a factor of any importance, even if proved, because if this is in truth the proper clue to the story's meaning and it is provided to us in its closing moments and with the necessity therefore on our part of relating it in retrospect to all that has gone before, we are at a loss to guess what purpose all the deliberately and elaborately worked out earlier sections of the story can be said to have served.[9] It is as if before Oedipus's downfall, Sophocles had insinuated as a complication or extenuation some human element—something, that is, that possibly could have forestalled the king's fate—and in so doing had vitiated the theme of inevitability, of inexorability that gives his play its terrible force.

If a not-to-be-denied death wish has brought about the Swede's death, then section 9 is irrelevant, an anticlimax and a puzzle; if, on the other hand, death resulted from the other men's non-involvement, then why was the death wish given so prominent a part? The two possible causes cannot merge or complement each other—this is the root of the trouble—they can, each one, only cancel the other. Crane may have had in mind the theme we identify with his other important work: when men are faced with danger and possible loss of life, their adversary is a formidable one. Witness the adversary war, in *The Red Badge*; witness the adversary ocean in "The Open Boat." Their strength then lies not in the Lord who made heaven and earth and who also made violence and death, but in each other. Charles Neider has written about Tolstoy, that from Schopenhauer "he inherited a shame of his Western singularity and he desired to tear away

that 'web of Maya' of which Schopenhauer so elo-
quently writes . . . , the solipsistic web which makes
each individual secretly believe in his immortality and
which prevents him from merging with his fellow
humans in a mental flow of utter communion." [10]
This is the web whose tearing away is accomplished by
Henry Fleming's fright, and the freedom from which
makes it possible for him to reach out to, touch hands
with, and rise to heights of fearlessness with, that
other frightened soldier, Wilson. This is the web that
awareness of the hitherto outrageous possibility of his
own death tears away from the correspondent of "The
Open Boat": now for the first time the dying soldier
in the sentimental boyhood poem becomes real to
him and deserving of his pity. So, perhaps, Crane is
saying in the story about the blue hotel, the Easterner's gradual recognition of the murderousness of the
elements outside Scully's hotel makes him aware of
the possibility that the Swede is not talking merely
fear-crazed nonsense; that this awareness serves to tear
away his veil; and the fact of his refusal or inability to
implement this awareness carries with it the heavy
burden of guilt that he confesses to the cowboy at the
end. But here the story can fit the theme only with
such contrivance as the Easterner is guilty of in his
curtain speech. For working against this theme is its
author's very success in portraying the Swede as a
victim of a true obsession, of morbid mania. The
difference between the Swede's relationship to his ac-
quaintances—which is to say, to the Easterner—and
the protagonist's relationship to his fellows in the
other two stories just cited makes the theme for once
inapplicable. How can we expect the Easterner or
anyone else in the story to feel implication in the fate
of a morbidly excited man, a man pursued by private
demons and sure to come to a violent end no matter

what collaboration of help the group in the hotel might employ?

Or perhaps the very fact of the Easterner's lecture on Collaboration is in truth the final irony, rather than the customarily identified one—namely, the explanation the lecture contains? If so, the only party initiate to the story's true meaning when it is over is not even the Easterner, but the reader. Surely that would be baffling and cryptic. Yet to fall back on any of the other interpretations is equally unsatisfactory. Thus the very inadequacy of any theory to reconcile apparently conflicting purposes persuades us of the aptness of Mr. Stallman's judgment that "The Blue Hotel" is constructed imperfectly and that it simply will not stand up under scrutiny.[11]

Supporting this conclusion is abundant evidence of unevenness and apparent indirection or improvisation in the story. Some of this relates to its plot, particularly of section 9. Granted that several months must be made to elapse for legal action to be taken on the stabbing, the fact of the Easterner's presence on the Dakota ranch when the sentence is announced arouses our curiosity. Why is he there? He is merely one of a group of three men who have come from the westbound train, who are strangers to each other, and who must lie over and then continue, presumably to separate destinations. There is nothing to suggest that Blanc and the cowboy were originally traveling together. In fact, Crane's introduction ("one was a tall bronzed cowboy, who was on his way to a ranch near the Dakota line; one was a little silent man from the East, who didn't look it, and didn't announce it") invites us to assume that they did not have a common destination. Then, too, the very circumstance that these two men have been living together for months after the stabbing renders implausible Blanc's withholding this (to him) truth from his close companion. Surely Blanc could have told the cowboy the truth the next morning, once they had left the blue hotel and he could speak his mind without constraint (and once he had freed himself from the spell it had cast over him too). Furthermore, a lecture stemming from a recent surge of self-guilt feelings (which one critic has charted) could be more climactically delivered the next day than months later. Finally, since, as the cowboy points out, it was a rather light sentence that the gambler received in any event, possibly Crane weakens rather than heightens his climax by delaying it until the exact sentence can be published.

More important as evidence of Crane's failure to control the materials of his story is his characterization of old Scully, who figures integrally during the greater part of the story's action. To scrutinize the part he is given is to be impressed with the same apparent puzzles as in the final direction of "The Blue Hotel" itself; in fact, the story's end leaves only conflicting clues to his basic identity. For Scully is not even one person but two people practically unreconcilable. The first and more frequent is a proud and benevolent, but also jovial, dialectal, and even comic Irishman straight out of the Bowery pages of E. W. Townsend, Richard Harding Davis, or Peter Finley Dunne. And he is so characterized, we have good reason for believing, for the purpose of contrasting with and heightening the sense of mystery and foreboding represented by the Swede, for whom he is evidently the main foil. As a result, there is a richly comic tone in the first scenes, which he almost succeeds in stealing from the morbidly apprehensive Swede. He is introduced as a "master of strategy" in devising an outlandish paint color to attract the attention and patronage of transient train passengers. Crane characterizes him as one who can "work his seductions" on any "wavering" passenger. He

"catches" three men; he "practically made them pris-
oners." He is a nimble, merry, kindly, "eager little
Irishman." And he looks comic, too, for he wears his
cap squeezed down so tightly on his head that "his
two red ears . . . stuck out stiffly as if they were made
of tin." He benevolently dispenses towels to his new
guests "with an air of philanthropic impulse." He
affectionately offers the Swede a drink from a lovingly
hoarded bottle that has escaped his son's inroads and
his wife's confiscation! And let us not forget that
when the two men descend, Scully too is drunk, is
"flushed and anecdotal."

As such, he is an important figure in the story. Since
"The Blue Hotel" is first and last the portrayal of a
region as it appears, weirdly distorted, to the mind of
a morbid stranger, for a full understanding of that
distortion we must have a variety of evidence, from
other sources, of the comparative safety and harmlessness of this region, of its essential kinship to the
comfort and safety of the more civilized regions of the
country, in particular of the East, which is the Swede's
home. This Crane has carefully and most effectively
provided. Here is a stove that roars welcome, warmth,
and protection from the violence of the elements.
Here is a laconic, relaxed, bored native cowboy. Here
is civilization incarnate: a family consisting of a boy,
girls, and wife—and more than all else, an eager,
friendly, merry, bespectacled, evening-newspaper-read-
ing, henpecked immigrant, from the East himself,
with talk of streetcars and other municipal improve-
ments in the spring! We recognize in his characterization as deliberate an exaggeration of the inherent ami-
ability, of the harmlessness, of the West as the
Swede's visions of it (and of him!) are of its harmful-
ness; and he is so created for our and the Swede's
benefit.

As is—once the story moves from the blue hotel to the saloon—the little gambler who finally kills him: a peaceable, respected husband, father, and entrepreneur, well thought of by his equally respectable cronies (a district attorney and two merchants) and with "a neat cottage in a suburb." Like Scully he qualifies for membership in a Better Business Bureau at Romper; like the tiny Scully he, however, assumes fearful possibilities in the eyes of the "burly" drink- and fear-crazed Swede. In the same way, to quiet the excitable and self-accusing mind of the young recruit in *The Red Badge*, to present war in all of its aspects, Crane had introduced a kindly, mellowing, life-nurturing sun to balance the one that gorges on blood; and the easy, yet non-cowardly (Smithers) way out of the cannon's reach to balance the stoic martyrdom of Jim Conklin. (The general in *The Red Badge*, who looks like a businessman reacting to a discouraging market report or who in the heat of battle reminds an orderly not to forget that box of cigars, is a reminder to us in turn and to Henry Fleming of the many casual, prosaic, lulling aspects of battle, to balance Henry's and our vision of those weird imps tending those weird and fearful animals called cannon.) Crane's talent is not ordinarily for comedy, but occasionally in "The Blue Hotel" it is impressively displayed.

Scully can, of course, be serious, as when he keeps Johnnie's antagonism in check or tries patiently to allay the Swede's fears upstairs. But the other Scully, to whom the first almost needs introduction, is an old man whose face the proper light can transform into that of a somber, mysterious personage. In the bedroom, "Scully's wrinkled visage showed grimly in the light of the small lamp he carried. This yellow effulgence, streaming upward, colored only his prominent features, and left his eyes, for instance, in mysterious shadow. He resembled a murderer." Sitting (again, note, in the lamplight) with spectacles and newspaper, he has "an appearance curiously like an old priest." And Crane even insists that outdoors his face, "in the subtly luminous gloom, could be seen set in the austere impersonal lines that are pictured on the countenances of the Roman veterans."

Worse yet, in all these views we detect no progression, no necessary index to the steady and rapid deterioration of the Swede's mental balance, for the two Scully characterizations do not metamorphose one into the other. In fact, they alternate. In *Maggie*, the drunken and disgusting Pete is momentarily represented—for no visible purpose other than impressionism—as drawing bills from his pocket and offering them to one of his drinking partners, Nell, "with the trembling fingers of an offering priest." Conversely, in "The Blue Hotel" the "old priest" above suddenly and almost comically catches his spectacles in mid-air as they fall at the sound of the Swede's accusation; and the "iron-nerved" and "austere" Roman-veteran referee of section 6 yields to the comic Irishman singing a duet of bravado-mortification with the cowboy in section 7; so that he leaves Crane's stage as he entered it, a comic chameleon. Crane thus failed here. Chiaroscuro replaced consistency, and art gave way to impressionism. As Crane's main and pervasive purpose in the story collapsed, we see, his supporting artistry collapsed with it.

The Crane who wrote *The Red Badge of Courage* had many materials for his story, and complete control of all of them. The Crane who wrote "The Blue Hotel," however, had two themes to present: one, the inevitable demoralization and disintegration of a morbidly excited mind at its initiation into what it takes to be the actively malevolent fierceness of the men and the weather of the prairies; the other, man's inhumanity to man, the influence of the equally grievous sins of omission and commission on the direction of human destiny. In trying to make his lecture on ethics —or simply letting it become—an overlay or extension of an analysis of the hero's mind, Crane left his readers with no theme at all.

But to put it another way, "The Blue Hotel" does not fail until after it has already succeeded. Crane was anticipating Picasso in heightening psychological effect with the use of blue (while at the same time simply continuing in the literary tradition of Poe and Melville); and I do not know of a later attempt at presenting progressive mental deterioration within so brief a medium that comes off this well unless it is Eugene O'Neill's *Emperor Jones* or *The Hairy Ape*. These, of course, have the advantage of the theater's expressionistic techniques for presenting inner states that were unavailable to Crane; as was, practically speaking, the technique of stream of consciousness, psychology's contribution to fiction. But only five years later, Crane's Swede was followed by Henry James's "The Beast in the Jungle," whose morbidly self-concerned hero-victim also senses and even invites a horrible fate; who has from his "earliest time . . . the sense of . . . something . . . possibly prodigious and terrible, that was sooner or later to happen to [him], . . . and that would perhaps overwhelm [him]." With John Marcher we watch the passage of the years, awaiting in a dread of inactivity his aweful destiny and like him wondering only what particular shape the terrible thing will take. It is only a momentary surprise to read that after the Redskin Stephen Crane left his homeland and found as a neighbor in Sussex, England, his country's most distinguished Paleface, Henry James, the two expatriates took to each other at once. They were, after all, tillers in the same soil.

5

Robert Frost

A century after Herman Melville had called the attention of the readers of the nation to a deep and disturbing theological principle in Nathaniel Hawthorne's short stories that might have escaped their notice, a prominent critic stood up in the same city to render a similar service to the metaphysics at the root of Robert Frost's poetry. Frost was, Lionel Trilling insisted, not a poet "who reassures us by his affirmation of old virtues . . . and ways of feeling" but a "terrifying" poet whose poetry conceives a "terrifying" universe: "The manifest America of Mr. Frost's poems may be pastoral; the actual America is tragic." [1] Perhaps nowhere is this disparity between apparently placid pensiveness about nature and deep down terror more memorably displayed than in the poem "Spring Pools." Equally important, the unreason, the promptings of the heart that cloud the poet's mind here, the frenzy that the poem lays bare is for once the outcome of thinking too long and too curiously, not about the appalling and deadening fury of winter's snow, but of summer's leaves.

Is it to exaggerate at all to say that this little poem about water and flowers and trees is actually about none of these, except as they represent what the poem is really about? We realize this certainly by the time we reach line 9, where in "Let them think twice" the poet directly identifies the trees with something that possesses the power of thought—in short, with human beings. To be sure, any poet could address (and count-less have addressed) non-cognitive organisms simply by exercising that part of their poetic license that applies to Pathetic Fallacy. And although Robert Frost himself is by no means averse to just such a practice, he is not merely poetizing here. The mode of his verb (let them) is blunt and sullen enough to be proof of this. And when we look back at the first stanza, our intuition is confirmed. For just as here, in stanza 2, the trees are meant to be thought of as humans, so back there, the pools and flowers in being described as chilled, as shivering, had also been hu-mans. If to this one objects that this is merely further evidence that the entire poem is an exercise in Pa-thetic Fallacy, the only reply can be that if it is, the poem would not be worth the effort it cost to write it. For what would it then say, if its meaning is merely literal? Simply that trees should not be rash in exercis-ing their power to eliminate the pools of water in early spring and the flowers that these pools have given birth to. Why? Because—for some undisclosed reason —early spring is dearer to the poet than midsummer is; because lightness in natural scenery is preferable to darkness; the fragile, to the dense.

Now, permissible poetically though this be, it is simply velleity, whim, diaphanous and too poetically pretty to be respected. We sense from the start that more is here, and from immersion in the poem's depths—the poem, like a pool of clearest water, turns out to be far deeper than it seems from the surface— we come to an awareness of just how much more that is: the poem is about nothing less than life and death, and about the only human measure by which we compute the passage from the beginning of one to the other—namely, time. *Only yesterday*. Essential to our understanding of this highly charged cry from the soul's depths is the very last line of the poem. Yet this periodic structure in no way lessens the effect that the preceding lines have had on us. We recall, after the last line (12), its foreshadowing that Frost had provided back in line 4 (soon); and the effect is, in any event, cumulative: as usual with good poetry, we are being led to the poem's meaning by implication and suggestion (as well as by verbal guideposts such as these two referred to).

There are at least two ways to draw a narrower and narrower circle of definition of the two complementary yet inimical aspects of life that constitute this poem's basic antithesis. One way is Frost's other poems. "Reluctance" too is about the change of seasons, here not from early spring to midsummer but from summer to autumn. Summer has died, and the poet wistfully contemplates the leaves lying dead on the ground, the withered stalks of flowers, and confesses that it is against human nature to "yield . . . to reason" and accept the alteration in the face of nature, to "bow and accept the end / Of a love or a season." We should remember the remark about the unreason of the poet's unwillingness to consent to the inexorable flight of time; otherwise, the poem is merely a delicate expression of melancholy wistfulness. As is "October." Here Frost pleads with this month to go slowly, not suddenly. But Frost's explanation of the two aspects of human existence that are opposed in "Spring Pools" can be found separately in yet two others of his poems, which if joined would state (directly, instead of almost covertly) the meaning of "Spring Pools." The first of these is "Nothing Gold Can Stay." In this epigram-like little poem, with its eight lines and forty words (most of them monosyllables—a measure of the poem's impetuousness), we are reminded of the account in Bede's history of the

Conversion of Edwin, in whose plaintive, melodic company it indeed belongs. The swallow that after its flight in from the cold, wintry night, tarries only a moment in the warmth and light of the mead-hall before its flight back into the cold and the dark, is transformed in Frost's poem into another symbol of evanescence—into the color and the substance of gold. For the more familiar symbol of the first evidence of life in the new natural year, which Hawthorne had spoken of as "a beautiful and tender green, to which no future luxuriance can add a charm," [2] Frost has substituted the conceit of the golden growths (crocus? marigold? forsythia?) that are spring's "first green" and whose early leaf is a flower (which leaf in turn subsides to leaf, he tells us in a mournful play on words). Six times during the course of the poem's eight separate and terse statements Frost mourns the golden flower's loss, disappearance, decline, or death; so that what emerges is a monody lamenting the breathless briefness of whatever perfect beauty this experience on earth provides: whether the perfection imagined in the pagan myth of the Golden Age (from which all subsequent ages have declined); or in the Judaeo-Christian myth of the Garden of Eden (from which we "sank to grief," to the pain and sweat of mortality); or finally in the decline of each day from the perfection of its golden dawn. Only one other perfection remains, and if we would see this in verse before Frost's day we should look in Shakespeare's song, where it is applied to the beauty of human youth:

> *Golden lads and girls all must,*
> *As chimney-sweepers, come to dust.*

Or in his sonnet, where he had conveyed the same message more literally, that "everything that grows /

Holds in perfection but a moment." Here nine words state the same truth as the title and four final words of "Nothing Gold Can Stay," and both describe the scene of the first of the two stanzas of "Spring Pools."

For an explanation of the change, of the disappearance or transformation of this first, golden green, which its second stanza concerns itself with, we should turn to another poem of Frost's, "Once By the Pacific." Containing no mention at all of the change of season as all of the others referred to above do, this poem asks us to see through the poet's eyes the quality of force, of violence (even rage) that Nature is capable of, that is a basic part of its nature. Here it takes the form of the towering waves: the water is even shattered, is broken. This then is merely another, more tangible, face of the same kinetic force that just as violently—if invisibly, and apparently statically—eradicates (blots out, drinks up, and sweeps away) the dear, delicate, first lucid shimmer of spring water and its companion, golden flowers. When Frost speaks of the trees having it in their pent-up buds, he is referring to an equally invisible yet equally tremendous force, such as we see the results of (for like the wind, this force can not be seen itself by the eye) in the thick slabs of concrete pavement that have been pushed up inches or a foot or more from their original place by the roots of trees expanding. Like the wind, or like water, as Frost reflects in "Two Tramps in Mud Time," don't forget

> *The lurking frost in the earth beneath*
> *That will steal forth after the sun is set*
> *And show on the water its crystal teeth.*

Since darkness not only seldom appears in Frost's poetry as merely a literal image of non-lightness but means something different almost every time he uses it, we must pause a little to perceive precisely what darkness means in the poem "Spring Pools." The darkness in "Mending Wall" that the neighbor is spoken of as moving in, is the darkness of mindlessness—a mental emptiness that does not so much think as parrot inherited adages. And when to this awareness we add the image Frost creates of a man carrying stones "like an old-stone savage armed," we realize that the darkness is that of the beginning of life on this earth, of emptiness when darkness ruled over the face of the waters, of the time when man first appeared and had a well-developed body but not as yet the power to think. Nor is the darkness of "Spring Pools" that of "Stopping By Woods," where it is both the lovely darkness of death, with its release from worldly responsibilities, and the unlovely darkness of life, of the shortest day of the year and therefore the one most conducive to the spiritual vagrancy that comes with the end of daylight. Still different is the darkness of "Once By the Pacific." Here the night of dark intent that Frost sees in the oncoming waves is an apocalyptic vision—a prophecy of some imminent alteration of the world's society, of something hidden and sinister—that he may be asking us to think of in the terms of St. John.

In "Spring Pools" the darkness that the dense foliage of the fully matured midsummer trees creates is nothing less than a force—like ocean waves—that obliterates the clear beauty of the peaceful nature-in-repose that the poet finds dear to his own peace of mind. And although to the average walker in the summer woods the dark foliage is a cooling and therefore welcome experience, to Frost it is a reminder of what this foliage has destroyed in order to come into being, namely

these flowery waters and these watery flowers
From snow that melted only yesterday.

And all this complex connection of ideas is conveyed to readers of "Spring Pools" by one or two words, a suggestion here and there. We respond to them and soon sense that although we cannot put our understanding into exactly the words we need, still we are attuned to the poet's thoughts because of his symbols.

The other help to understanding "Spring Pools" comes from German philosophy. A century and more ago Arthur Schopenhauer presented his view of our world as composed of Will and Idea. Nature was a nature of force, of will power, basically sexual and serving thereby the needs of nature—the overriding concern of creation. Man was a helpless victim of this thing-in-itself, this fierce will, until and when he could detach himself from it by a deliberate act of abnegation, self-denial, by freeing himself from this force. Such was possible, he said, by the act of recognition, by contemplation of man's human condition. This act of recognition was in itself an accomplishment of idea, which thereby—and only thereby—transcended the all-powerful will of nature. His disciple Nietzsche embraced and modified Schopenhauer's thesis in advancing, in *The Birth of Tragedy*, what he called his "metaphysics for artists." Here the earlier terms emerge as the Apollonian and the Dionysian aspects of human nature. Nietzsche saw Apollo as the transfiguring genius of the *principium individuationis* through which alone the redemption in appearance is truly to be obtained; while by the mystical triumphant cry of Dionysus the spell of individuation is broken and the way lies open to . . . the innermost heart of things." It was the fusion, the combination of these usually parallel and opposed forces (one asserting the individuality, the other denying and submerging it in universality) that resulted in the birth of Greek drama. The Apollonian, or contemplative, he saw finding plastic expression, in sculpture; the Dionysian, or drunken, dynamically in music.

Can we not see Robert Frost, in his turn, changing yet not importantly denying Nietzsche's terms, while returning to Schopenhauer's earlier vision of their essential separateness? Does he not present a world symbolized, instead of by sculpture and music, by the (1) spring pools, delicate flowers, and clear sky, and (2) the water-drunken roots, dense foliage, and darkness? Certainly his vision of the calm, immobile, and fragile world of early spring is a statuesque tableau; and his force that darkens nature in midsummer strongly suggests the Dionysian that to one earlier thinker symbolized sexual force, and to the other, drunkenness and music. "Thus does the Apollonian tear us away from Dionysian universality and make us delight in individuals; . . . the Apollonian influence uplifts man from his orgiastic self-annihilation."—if we stop here, short of the completion of the Nietzschean metaphysic of drama, we have, I think, found a close enough parallel to Frost's vision to throw light on it. In this vision no fusion, no merging, is proposed. Frost maintains a careful separation of these warring constituents of the human condition in nature and arrives, not at a tragic view, but at one of pained longing intensified by a premonition of its being vanquished by the other, and invisible, force. He keeps separate in his mind the peace and delicacy and clearness of spring pools and spring flowers and opposes them to the force and darkness of summer woods. These last are the midsummer madness of human life, the upsurging, the frenzied release, the thing-in-itself of Schopenhauer, the orgiastic torrent of Euripides' *Bacchae* which sweeps all before it, the unreason of our inmost beings. We can find other statements of these antithetical or complementary factors in the drama of human life both before and after Frost's statement of it. Freud's employs the psychoanalytical terms of ego and id. The ego functions to bring "the influence of the external world to bear upon the id and its tendencies," and tries "to substitute the reality-principle for the pleasure-principle which reigns supreme in the id. In the ego perception plays the part which in the id devolves upon instinct. The ego represents what we call reason and sanity, in contrast to the id which contains the passions." [3] Albert Camus later transposed Frost's terms into those of existential philosophy. A day comes, he writes, "when a man notices or says that he is thirty. Thus he asserts his youth. But simultaneously he situates himself in relation to time. He takes his place in it. He admits that he stands at a certain point on a curve that he acknowledges having to travel to its end. He belongs to time, and by the horror that seizes him, he recognizes his worst enemy. Tomorrow, he was longing for tomorrow, whereas everything in him ought to reject it. The revolt of the flesh is absurd." [4]

To review what we have been told by the poem: the most beautiful period of our life is its youth, just as its cognate, Spring, is the loveliest of our year's seasons (the golden one). It suddenly appears, as it were, from nowhere (melted snow) and in its pride and strength it hastens to assert itself, not pausing—in its strength—to reflect that what came quickly also goes quickly; that if it itself arose from snow that melted only yesterday, it will be rash to speed its own vigorous pursuit of maturity, because this too will speed by, and age will contemplate wistfully the maturity that seemed to come only yesterday. Only as a low relief on a Grecian urn in the poem can the youth forever be within a hand's grasp of his beloved; in real life, no time is arrested, all life passes in a flash. The charm of the maiden in the scene on the antique urn is that she is as yet unravished (like the urn) and for that reason will always retain her purity of vision while retaining her virginity. The charm of the pools in the spring and of their flowers is that of a fragile and delicate purity that will, alas, suddenly be gone (except on the sculptured urn, where the happy, happy boughs need never bid the Spring adieu), giving way to a sexual release that, while it brings with it a power resulting from knowingness about the ways of nature, yet will do so at the expense of ravishing the earlier purity. (In the northern part of our country, the middle-aged Hawthorne had reflected from gentler Italy, Spring bursts into Summer with "headlong haste"; "the virgin Spring hastens to its bridal," into "married Summer" much "too abruptly.") [5]

Let eager, proud, importunate youth reflect on this, and it will not be so quick to cast off its innocence and serenity—its clear, unclouded vision that reflects its celestial origin before shades of the prison house close in upon it. Lucidity and repose are the price youth pays for the strength of maturity; manhood brings with it darkness and turmoil. And, eventually, death. What wonder, then, that Frost implores, threatens, with his "Let them think twice"? (With far greater detachment, Hawthorne had made the same observation: "Summer works in the present, and thinks not of the future.") [6] How could he do less?

Artistically, the poem is equally remarkable, written, as it seems to be, by a poet with a command of rhetoric and music. The tone of its music, we discover, supports the message of its words.

The first of the two stanzas is about the pools; the

second, about the trees. The first, then, belongs to the protagonist; the second, to the antagonist. Neatly balanced though this is, there is yet another, a secondary, balance or antithesis. We note that the closing line of the first stanza ends with the ominous appearance of the antagonist (roots, dark foliage—*i.e.*, midsummer) who will dominate the second stanza. Correspondingly, the last lines of this second stanza re-introduce the now-vanquished antagonist of the first stanza (flowery waters, watery flowers). This completes the symmetry, almost the choreography, for it directs the poem to an ending that is its beginning. This theme of conflict, of opposition of two exactly balanced forces, is further underscored by the parallel syntactical construction of the two stanzas. Simply stated, in the first stanza, the first words give us the subject (pools) of the sentence that occupies the entire six lines of the stanza; yet this subject does not receive its verb until the fourth line, when the stanza is half ended. Similarly, in the second stanza, the subject (trees) appearing in the first line does not receive its verb until the third line. The only thing, rhetorically speaking, that keeps the second construction from exactly repeating the first is the abrupt shift in mode; for in line 3 the second stanza suddenly becomes injunctive, hortatory. And fittingly: whereas the simple declarative form of stanza 1 is in keeping with its elegiac message, the intensity of the poet's resentment at the power of the victorious adversary unreason is best expressed by the minatory, by the hortative mode. Thus do we, past the *mezzo del cammin di nostra vita*, warn, protest against the madness that we have lived through, entreating, threatening youth: "Resist, desist! As we did not!" They will not, to be sure; but mere expressions about folly to them would avail even less.

Not that "Spring Pools" is perfect, artistically

speaking. In fact, its blemishes are prominent and, worse yet, they appear early in the poem. Yet this diminishes the poem's effect hardly at all—our most convincing proof of the strength and greatness of the whole. In a poem so brief, the unfortunate sequence in line 1 of two consecutive subordinating conjunctions (that, though) is almost ruinous, psychologically and melodically as well. Also, the construction stares at us in its bookish, glaringly grammatical formality. Actually, the poem gets off in its first four words to a singularly poor start, for three of them (These . . . that, though) are uses of one palatal sound itself not particularly adaptable to lyric poetry. Recovering from this, we again halt, in line 2, at a bookish, intellected indirection (almost without), a litotes understandable chiefly on the grounds of rhyme, and therefore a little obtrusive. Continuing now at this stumbling pace, we pause in line 3 at chill and shiver, where we do not instantly grant the poet the apposition of the two verbs. Is chill what it has always been—either transitive verb or noun or adjective? After shiver, we realize that it is a verb after all; but instead of recovering, we simply recover our uneasiness and our objections: Frost has given us a coinage, using chill as an intransitive verb, as a synonym for are chilly. But this is all. The poem quickly recovers its momentum and does not lose it after that. From the very beginning, moreover, it is a virtuoso's collection of poetic effects, a sonata first for flute and then for bass viol which modern lyric poetry seldom equals.

We may marvel, for instance, at the daring repetition, word for word, of the greater part of a line in two consecutive lines (3 and 4) in a poem only twelve lines long. Then we recognize it as an emphasized identification of flowers with pools. These two entities are exactly contemporaneous—even in terms of days, hours—and are the one (flowers) the result of the other (pools). Frost's repetition here, then, differs in purpose from that of the closing lines of the equally brief "Stopping By Woods," which provides a fine closing cadence and emphasizes the weariness present and contemplated of all the obligations in life before rest (death). This association of two early spring fellows in brief beauty is revived with a different metaphor toward the end in "these flowery waters and these watery flowers." The emphasis receives reinforcement in the reference, in lines 1 and 11, to the pools and flowers as "these." Conversely, Frost uses "the" in the important opening line (7) of the second stanza to refer to trees because they are not the protagonist, but merely the antagonist. Certainly "these" would fit equally well otherwise.

But by all means the most striking effect of "Spring Pools" is its reliance, for its important kinetic effects, not on verbs, but on prepositions. With this poem is the verb dethroned; no longer can we think of using only it to convey important action. Isn't "Spring Pools" the most prepositional lyric poem in our literature? The sheer number, fourteen (eight in the first stanza; six in the second)—by it Frost seems to be demonstrating the variety and versatility of the compound of verb and preposition. Never before, possibly, has the effect of vigor or force been so completely conveyed by this part of speech. Notice the static "in" of line 1 and the "beside" of lines 3 and 4. These express, and they express exactly, the static condition that Frost holds dear. But then in line 5 the "out" conveys the first idea of action, of obliterating force, followed by the "up" in line 6. And the "on" which is the very last word of the stanza is a surprising choice. Frost forces it on our attention by his violation of the grammar etiquette which forbids its use there; yet this is exactly to his purpose, because it introduces the sinister power which the second stanza (which follows this word "on" immediately) is devoted to—namely, the on-ness, the fullness, the fruition, the completeness of the darkness that Frost fears, the riot against reason; the pestilence, that is, that worketh in the noonday of man's life.

Yet, powerful as these prepositions (or verb-preposition combinations) are, they merely prepare us for the avalanche that pours down over us in the last half of the second stanza. The first warning sound of this is in the stanza's first line, with its "pent-up," which is by itself the most powerful of all the combinations in the poem. It contains the poet's sense of an ominous compression in nature. Pen something in or up and you are vainly trying to frustrate the inevitable, if not increasing the volume of the not-to-be-denied force which eventually will be released. As it is in line 10, where it overwhelms the reader, as it does the helpless flowers, which it blots out and drinks up and finally, utterly sweeps *away*.

Their death is mourned in music. Earlier, particularly in the first stanza, we had discovered from reading the poem aloud, that melodious as the various end rhymes are, there is another music within the lines. Almost consecutively in the first four lines we have the succession of liquid notes in still, then chill, then will. And at the other end of the stanza, roots follows brook. So too now, at the close of the poem, the passing—actually, the destruction—of the pools and the flowers is annotated with the fitting elegiac music of the final lines, with the keening, the *ululatu* of the sounds *ay* (away, yesterday) and *aw* (waters, watery) and *oh* (snow, only) that faintly echo the mournful groans of Milton's sonnet on the slaughtered Piemontese. An exquisite requiem for the passing of nature's first born!

In a Zola novel an old peasant woman shakes her fists in rage at the heavens disgorging the hail that is ruining her crops; and in a Stephen Crane story the correspondent wants to maim the deity that has presided over his shipwreck. But these affronts to our prosperity and threats to our life are only freaks of nature's violence. In Frost's poem all of us live to mourn an inner, universal misfortune. Looking out and back in middle age, we contemplate the limpid beauty of youth now gone, knowing that there hath past away a glory from our lives; and from our cells in his keep, we still rattle the chains thrust on us by the giant Unreason.

6

William Faulkner

For some years now it has been convenient and profitable, in studying William Faulkner's "A Rose for Emily," to follow the suggestion offered by Professors Brooks and Warren in *Understanding Fiction* that we consider it in comparison with Poe's "The Fall of the House of Usher," on the grounds that in both "we have a decaying mansion in which the protagonist, shut away from the world, grows into something monstrous." This notwithstanding the fact that to do so— as these critics more or less admit—is to point up as many differences as similarities. While it is indisputable that each is "a story of horror," the gloomy corridors of Gothicism are too numerous for such a suggestion to prove more than initially instructive.

Without discarding the Brooks-Warren approach, let us extend it and consider Faulkner's spirit-chilling little classic along the additional lines proposed more recently by Professor Randall Stewart. Faulkner, he reminds us, "had certain important lineal relations, as a writer, to the regional literature which preceded him. . . . Faulkner's relation to his Southern predecessors . . .—a whole new field—has scarcely been studied at all." In particular, let us compare "A Rose for Emily" with George Washington Cable's "Jean-ah Poquelin," a musty, ghoulish little tale of old New Orleans originally published in 1879 in *Old Creole Days*, long very popular, but now seldom exhumed. Close inspection will reveal that Faulkner's story is more akin to Cable's not only in the canon of horror, but in that far more important quality defined by Professor Stewart as "a common view of the human condition." Although the situations of these two stories are curiously similar, they are productive of dissimilar results. To compare them along with Poe's is to arrive at some interesting discoveries about the changing function that Gothic fiction has served during the past century in its presentation of the human personality. Particularly, it is to observe that familiar Gothic stock-in-trade, the recluse, in the process of emerging from his original confines of physical and psychic isolation, shielding from us some suspected hidden horror, into a flesh-and-blood person harboring no horror so real as that of the deterioration of his mind. What gives Faulkner's story its great claim to our admiration is not that he has created an individual who becomes insane, but that he places her in our midst and makes us believe in her. With "A Rose For Emily" morbidity is domesticated in the American small town.

Like "Usher," Cable's and Faulkner's are stories of horror, but unlike it, they are everywhere stories of time and place. Cable sets this down in his first sentence and Faulkner devotes an entire early paragraph to it. Our imagination is thus fixed at once in both stories on an exact setting. Professor Randall Stewart has pointed out that "a rampant industrialism was transforming the traditional social structure" of the South in the 1920's;[1] similarly, in the years immediately following 1803, the somnolent French province of Louisiana was asked to adapt itself to the American ways of progress. "In the first decade of the present century," Cable begins, matter-of-factly; yet further on we see that this detail is important: merely a decade or two later, during the flood of American immigration into New Orleans, Poquelin's interview with the Governor would have been pathetic, rather than dramatic; and even a decade earlier, there would have been no need for it (the purchase of Louisiana in 1803 being ultimately responsible for Poquelin's desperate situation). Similarly, the coming of garages and gasoline pumps mentioned in the beginning of Faulkner's story places us squarely in the Jefferson of the 1910's and 1920's—a seemingly casual fact that becomes indispensable: it was this change wrought on American life by technology that resulted in the paving of small-town sidewalks and streets, which in turn brought the Yankee suitor to Jefferson. And thereby hangs Faulkner's tale. Into both settings of change the author introduces a hero who, fortifying himself in an anachronistic, horrible yet majestic stronghold, ignores or defies the insistent encroachments of time and progress. It is in the manner in which Poquelin and Miss Emily oppose these encroachments that their creators show their kinship and, after all, their basic difference.

Each curtain goes up on an isolated fortress from bygone days. Jean-ah's is an ancient structure masterfully invested by Cable with all the forbidding attributes of a decaying medieval castle, complete even with moat. This "old colonial plantation-house" in New Orleans "half in ruin," stands "aloof from civilization" at some distance from the smaller, newer houses on the bank of the Mississippi. It is "grim, solid, and spiritless," "its massive build" a reminder of an earlier, more hazardous period of American history. With its "dark" and "weather-beaten" roof and sides, it stands above a marsh in whose center grow two dead cypresses, "clotted with roosting vultures." The Grierson home of Faulkner's story is similarly detached, superseded, and forbidding. It is a "big, squarish frame house that had once been white, decorated with cupolas and spires and scrolled balconies in the heavily lightsome style of the seventies." It too stands alone on the street as a human dwelling, "lifting its stubborn and coquettish decay above the cotton wagons and the gasoline pumps—an eyesore among eyesores."

In the first of these half-ruined homes lives a half-ruined old creole grandee, "once an opulent indigo planter, . . . now a hermit, alike shunned by and shunning all who had ever known him," the last of a prominent Louisiana line. His only relative, a much younger half-brother named Jacques, has not been seen for seven years, two years after "Jean-ah" (Jean Marie) and he left for the Guinea coast on a slave-capturing expedition and Jean-ah returned alone. ("He must have arrived at his house by night. No one saw him come. No one saw 'his little brother'; rumor whispered that he, too, had returned, but he had never been seen again.") This livelihood Poquelin had descended to after his indigo fields had had to be abandoned, and, after that, smuggling. At the time of Jacques' disappearance there was suspicion of foul play, and with the passing of the years old Jean-ah's name has become "a symbol of witchery, devilish crime, and hideous nursery fictions." His society is avoided, and boys playing in the neighborhood jibe at the old man, who retaliates imperiously with violent but outdated and unheeded "French imprecation and invective." All avoid the house after dark. So far as anyone knows, Poquelin lives only with an old African housekeeper, who happens to be a mute.

Emily Grierson is a similarly pathetic yet sinister relic. The last of a proud line, she lives on in her outmoded stronghold, alone but peremptory in her demand for "recognition of her dignity as the last

Grierson." Since her father's death she has lived all alone in the big house except for a brief period in her thirties when she went off with a Yankee construction foreman named Homer Barron, presumably to be married. Her lover has since disappeared. ("[Within] three days Homer Barron was back in town. A neighbor saw the Negro man admit him at the kitchen door at dusk one evening. And that was the last we saw of Homer Barron.") For a period of six or seven years, at the age of forty, Miss Emily deigns to teach china-painting as a source of income. Then, as years and the fashion pass and her pupils disappear, her front door is "closed upon the last one and remained closed for good." She lives on into old age in the house "filled with dust and shadows," a place associated in her townsmen's eyes with an unspoken and mysterious horror. The only other inmate, we read, is an old Negro house servant, who, interestingly, does not utter a word during the course of the story.

Eventually, progress, in the form of municipal expansion, becomes old Poquelin's adversary. Surveyors give signs of running a new street close to his house and of draining the morass beside it. This we note, is a Poquelin reverse that the townspeople relish. Although they too oppose new streets, and will welcome engineering difficulties, their fearful scorn for Poquelin causes them to look approvingly upon his forcible return to the community. Jean-ah goes directly to the Governor, mustering for the occasion his tattered dignity and—after the Governor understandably declines to speak in the French tongue—his broken English. He pleads on the old, man-to-man basis of the past when informality and the importance of the name Poquelin would have made this kind of interview appropriate; does not incline to the Governor's official-sounding suggestion that he deal with the city authorities; and even proposes that the Governor intercede in person on his behalf with no less than the President. To the Governor's innocent query about the stories associated with his house, Poquelin haughtily refuses to answer, and then departs. The city official to whom the Governor has referred him knows no French either and deals with Poquelin through an interpreter. After this second rebuff, Poquelin swears abusively and leaves.

The new street is cut through, and houses go up near Jean-ah's, but still the ugly old ruin remains, to the growing exasperation of the townspeople. Now the newer arrivals plot to persuade, then coerce, the old man to build a new home. Their efforts are rebuffed firmly by Poquelin, who refuses to permit conversation about it with the president of a local Board recently organized. The townspeople renew their pressure on Poquelin and even threaten mob action (a charivari, they say). On the fateful night, however, they are thwarted, both by the efforts of one of their group (who on a secret visit to the house, becomes suspicious, among other things, of a revolting odor about the place), and by the death of Poquelin himself. His body is brought out of the house by the old African mute, followed by the long-missing Jacques, a leper whose existence he has successfully concealed from all for seven years. Hoisting the coffin on his shoulders, the Negro starts out toward leper soil, Jacques with him: the two "stepped into the jungle, disappeared and were never seen again."

Miss Emily is equally impervious to community pressure. Yet her shabbily majestic seclusion is also menaced by the passing of time and by progress. In young spinsterhood when her father dies she refuses for days to let the neighbors have the body. Two years later she dares to consort openly with the crude Yankee, Homer Barron. The neighbors try to thwart the relationship out of mixed feelings: they both resent Emily's haughtiness (she is insufferably Grierson, even when fallen on evil days) and yet actually sympathize with her (after all, she is one of them, as Homer is not, and the relatives whom they send for turn out to be "even more Grierson" than Emily). She defies the druggist by refusing to tell him why she is buying the arsenic. Shortly afterwards, when Homer apparently deserts her on the eve of their presumed wedding, and an offensive smell develops in her house, there is angry complaining to authority. But the old major intercedes in Emily's behalf, and the only community action that results is the sprinkling of lime around her house (secretly, almost fearfully, at night).

Times passes. She refuses to accept free postal delivery. Finally, thirty years later, when her continued refusals to pay her taxes cause the major himself to write a kind letter to her proposing payment, he "received in reply a note on paper of an archaic shape, in a thin, flowing calligraphy in fading ink" airily rebuffing his proposal. This imperiousness finally causes a deputation of townspeople (mostly younger) to call on her in her dusty, sinister-smelling domain. She turns them away haughtily, claiming an immunity to taxes based on a lifelong remission by a mayor long since dead, to whom she refers the deputation. When death finally comes to the old woman herself, the ancient Negro admits the first visitors to the house, then disappears: "He walked right through the house and out the back and was not seen again." The visitors enter it for the first time in ten years, break down a door abovestairs which no one has opened in forty years, and find the long-decayed corpse of her lover lying in the bed. Only after her death does the town discover the permanence of her conquest a generation before over a man who evidently had no intention of remaining true to her.

Here, then, are two stories presenting a central conflict between a last proud and doomed but indomitable representative of an important family of a bygone era of the South and an encroaching, usurping civilization. Both Emily Grierson and Jean-Marie Poquelin perpetuate their pristine importance by immuring themselves in a massive, impregnable, outmoded house; and both successfully conceal in that house until their death a human ghoul who is all that is left to them, the success of the concealment itself recording the triumph of a figure whom time and progress have otherwise relegated to ridiculousness. With plot and characterization parallels like these one might well speculate about the extent to which Cable's story may have inspired Faulkner's. Yet there is a surprising difference in the impressions these two stories create. For, after all the parallels have been itemized, Faulkner has used old materials in an entirely new way and created an effect that is neither Poe's nor even Cable's but entirely his own. To be sure, the effect is derived from the Gothic horror effects of the preceding centuries, but it is also characteristically modern and the more horrifying for that reason.

Cable's story itself is, of course, in the old tradition. The mysterious and forbidding ruin superseded by time, the proud and isolated owner, a hidden horror —these are the devices of Poe and his Germanic predecessors, long threadbare by Cable's time (had not Jane Austen's readers laughed at them long before Poe wrote his first word?). What distinguishes "Jean-ah Poquelin" from them is the fact that Cable has mixed in with his old Gothic colors fresh ones of local color and original characterization. The scene in which the old Frenchman confronts the governor of the new state of Louisiana is one of the memorable ones in our literature. And the stolid, valiant front old Poquelin presents to his suspicious and hostile neighbors over the years as he harbors a forbidden horror in his home at the risk of his own health is both a masterfully executed and a credible effect, taking place right on the lower Mississippi and as difficult to dissociate from it as Bret Harte's miners from the California gold fields or Edward Eggleston's circuit riders from southern Indiana or Harriet Beecher Stowe's Sam Lawson from New England or Harris' Negro story-teller from plantation Georgia. Moving in the opposite direction from Poe, whose addiction to European scenes and themes could cause him to transport even one of the all-too-scarce native revenge-murder plots from Kentucky to Rome, Cable has here succeeded in grafting the German plant onto a native one. With him the Gothic has received a local habitation and a name.

Yet, though "Jean-ah Poquelin" is a superior sort of melodrama, it cannot completely—or even largely— escape from the confines of that category. Poquelin's gloomy relic of a defunct creole colonialism, with the submarine horrors that guarantee its medieval isolation, is presented as an ugly obstacle to progress; yet, identify though we are encouraged to do with the new villas springing up around it and with the ways of that basically well-intentioned civic group, the "Building and Improvement Company" (one of whose officers, White, even becomes a secondary hero of the piece), primarily and consistently we sympathize with Poquelin and his heroic, if baffling, resistance to them. We do not willingly watch greatness, however faded, vanish from our view, and we all side against the instrument of its obliteration: as the moralist that his century required the serious writer of fiction to be, Cable had to inculcate in his readers attitudes of censure and approbation in viewing the opposing forces of the story.

Faulkner, on the other hand, impassively maintains his (and our) distance, sympathizing with and reproving in turn Emily and her adversary, the Town. The outmoded, mausoleum-like edifice from which she defies society is, to be sure, an eyesore, but to Faulkner it is merely "an eyesore among eyesores"—an unsightly dwelling in the midst of unsightly gasoline pumps. Between the boorish arrogance of Homer Barron and the cultured arrogance of Emily Grierson, can one choose? Or between the testy young alderman who does not recognize old ways and the crusty old judge who does not recognize new ones? Faulkner cares as little (or as much) for the "gross, teeming world" of the New South as he does for the one "monument" to the Old South whose identity it is effacing. His concern is not with the opposition of the forces of Good and Evil. In centering his inquiry on the workings of the morbid mind of his character, he moves beyond the terms of Cable.

Thus it is not surprising to reflect that, unlike Poe's and Cable's, Faulkner's Gothic story is not a suspense story at all. Our chief interest in "Usher" eventually focuses on the condition of the hero's sister and our curiosity is solely on what the outcome of the last horrible night will be. Almost to an equal degree Cable sets our minds to work on the mystery of Poquelin's insistence on seclusion and on the exact identity of the reported supernatural presence under his roof. Thus it is that when Poe's and Cable's living corpses at last emerge in their shrouds and the mystery of the central situational horror is solved, our minds have an answer—the lady Madeline and Jacques Poquelin had not really died—and need nothing more. Conversely, in "A Rose for Emily" not only do we early anticipate the final outcome with a fair degree of accuracy: for this very reason we are imbued with the horror of the heroine's personality at every step throughout the story, and thus in her case the basic mystery outlives the working out of the plot. For Faulkner, so far from withholding all clues to Homer Barron's whereabouts, scatters them with a precise prodigality; since his is a story primarily of character, it is to his purpose to saturate our awareness of Miss Emily's abnormality as he goes, so that the last six shocking words merely put the final touch on that purpose. They do not astound us or merely erase a question mark. If similarities to Faulkner are to be sought in Poe, they will be found not in "Usher," but in "A Cask of Amontillado," whose plot in no way parallels Faulkner's: both stories have a total horror, rather than a climax of horror, for in both we are given at the start a distinct impression of the moral depravity of the central figure, and the following pages deliberately heighten that impression rather than merely solve for us a mystery that the opening pages have set forth. We leave Miss Emily as awed by the complexity of her being as when we met her, and therein lies the greatness of Faulkner's story. With it the Southern Gothic has achieved the status of a serious art form.

But for the most striking evidence of the wide gulf that yawns between Faulkner and his Southern precursor Cable in horror fiction, of the two worlds in which they live, we must turn to the relationships of the two protagonists with their own dead (or living dead) and the effects these create in the reader. The strength of family ties of the Poquelins is emphasized early in Cable's story when we are told that even in old age Poquelin visits his father's tomb in St. Louis Cathedral daily. And we have abundant evidence of the cost of the heartrending tenderness with which Poquelin spends the years tending his leprous, decaying brother; for as Cable describes him in the interview with the governor, over his entire face is "the imprint of some great grief . . . faint but unmistakable." It clouds and weights his days and makes each breath a burden. And we, in turn, understand and are moved.

Compare with these conventional touches the effect of Change on Miss Emily. When we first inspect her house, in her old age, we merely note in passing that there is a portrait of her father "on a tarnished gilt easel before the fireplace" in the parlor. But when, during her early spinsterhood, her father dies and she refuses for three days to hand his putrefying body over for burial, we are shocked by this irrational action, even though in keeping with his standpoint of non-commitment Faulkner tries to minimize it ("We remembered all the young men her father had driven away, and we knew that with nothing left, she would have to cling to that which had robbed her, as people will"). Even more important, by Faulkner's time it was possible for him to defy taboo by substituting a husband for a brother (or, as in Usher's case, a sister) in the concealment theme. But the most frightening detail in Faulkner's story is this: not only does this obsessed spinster continue for some years to share a marriage bed with the body of the man she poisoned —she evidently derives either erotic gratification or spiritual sustenance (both?) from these ghastly nuptials. She becomes, in short, a necrophile or a veritable saprophytic organism; for we learn that the "slender figure in white" that was the young Miss Emily becomes, as though with the middle-aged propriety that the married state customarily brings, fat! "She looked bloated, like a body long submerged in motionless water, and that of parallel hue. Her eyes, lost in the fatty ridges of her face, looked like two small pieces of coal pressed into a lump of dough." It is in ghoulish inner evolutions like these that Faulkner moves beyond Poe and Cable into the twentieth century, directly into the clinic of Dr. R. von Krafft-Ebing, whose inquiries into the psychopathology of sex had revealed that "When no other act of cruelty . . . is practised on the cadaver, it is probable that the lifeless condition itself forms the stimulus for the perverse individual. It is possible that the corpse—a human form absolutely without will—satisfies an abnormal desire, in that the object of desire is seen to be capable of absolute subjugation, without possibility of resistance." [2]

Not that the appearance of the hero as pathological recluse had to await the present century, to be sure. But in "Usher" or other Poe tales the central character is patently offered to the reader and always received by him as a madman pure and simple; during the time we see him, he has never been sane; and his situation is never even remotely to be associated with ours—that is, with reality. Roderick Usher is, after all, a shadowy unknown living a bizarre existence in an unidentifiable land and time, and suffering from pale preoccupation with a body not-dead from an equally phantasmal ailment—all details of horror for horror's sake. [3]

Emily Grierson, on the other hand, not only has a local habitation and a name, she is someone we grow up with and old with. In fact, Faulkner's ubiquitousness and omniscience seem used deliberately for this purpose (at the expense of being an intrinsic artistic flaw in the story). Her relatives from Alabama and their relationship to the Mississippi Griersons are made much of, as are the careful distinctions between the various Protestant sects in the town. With the exception of the last ten years of her seventy-four, she is represented as living in a fairly familiar, understandable isolation for an aristocratic Southern woman, and demonstrating by the very success of her isolation the majesty and frightfulness of her position. For all that, like other Gothic characters, she is "impervious" and "perverse"—even to the point of madness—she is also "tranquil," "inescapable," even "dear." "All this happened, then," we say to ourselves at the close of her story, "in our very midst!" It happened, not in the Western Germany of several centuries ago, but in the Mississippi of yesterday. Although Faulkner's story is the "logical development" of Edgar Allan Poe, George Snell writes, "and at the same time shows his ineluctable kinship with Poe, as technician and as master of the morbid and bizarre," it is "brought to a higher degree of force since its action takes place not in some 'misty mid region' but exactly and circumstantially in a recognizable South, with all the appurtenances and criticisms of a society which Faulkner knows and simultaneously hates and loves." [4]

Furthermore, it would seriously detract from Faulkner's intention and achievement to limit our identification of Emily Grierson's pathological intransigence to the South alone. Appalling though Emily's dealings with the North (Homer Barron) are, far more attention is given to her resistance to her own townspeople. Thus Ray B. West, Jr.'s reminder that "The theme is not one directed at presenting an attitude of Southerner to Yankee. . . . The Southern problem is one of the objective facts with which the theme is concerned, but the theme itself transcends it"; and "Here is depicted the dilemma of our age, not of the South alone nor of the North alone." [5] If we need further evidence of this, can we not find it in the surname of the very heroine of Faulkner's story? So far from being one of Mississippi or even Southern association, it is that of none other than the officer in the Northern army who had led so celebrated and devastating a raid throughout the state of Mississippi midway through the Civil War! (And readers of Faulkner will recall how carefully he chooses names for his characters.) In this connection, we might let an eminent historian of the literary life in the United States call our attention to the eccentricities and grotesquerie of the population, both fictional and real, of the other areas of this country during Emily Grierson's decline—of the Midwest, of New England. What! we exclaim, emerging from a prolonged immersion in Faulkner—is this not Yoknapatawpha County, Mississippi?

> [It] abounded in men who had once been important and who had no life any longer to shape their code. . . . They had set the tone for their neighbours and headed their clans. But they had no clans to lead now, and the making of laws was not for them: they were left with the "dusty ruins of their fathers' dreams." They had lost their confidence, as the years went by, and they crept away into their houses and grew queerer and queerer. . . . There were creepers among catacombs, "whose occupation was to die," there were respected citizens who blew their brains out; and one saw them straggling through the town, stumbling over frozen ruts, in the cold white shine of a dreary day. In short, this population was a whole *Spoon River Anthology*, acting out its epitaphs in the world of the living.[6]

Actually, the town described above (Gardiner, Maine) is the world of an earlier American writer, Edwin Arlington Robinson. And when Amy Lowell wrote about another book that it "does not deal with the changed population, with the [immigrants] who are taking up the deserted farms. His people are left-overs of the old stock, morbid, pursued by phantoms, slowly sinking to insanity"—she could have been reviewing a Faulkner fiction instead of poetry by his contemporary, Robert Frost.[7]

We are left, then, with this irony: in order to identify exactly the weird wizardry that Faulkner has achieved in "A Rose For Emily," to distinguish it chiefly from Poe's, we must borrow a distinction that Poe himself claimed when he insisted that his particular brand of the Gothic was "not of the Rhine but of the soul."

"A Rose For Emily," George Snell has noted, "shows how little Faulkner has been restrained by the conventions of Southern life which have dictated to many Southern writers how little of reality they could deal with."[8] The necrophilia of that story, the nymphomania of *Light in August*—what other conventions were there for him to disregard?[9] Merely the most venerable of all to readers, the first and greatest dream, the Tale of Young Love. Briefly, to be sure, in an early part of *The Hamlet* we find ourselves in the old familiar world of popular fiction, reading, not about a putrefying suitor, but about a young man working his way through college by starring on the football field on weekends and teaching in a one-room country schoolhouse during the week who falls in love with one of his students. But as quickly as we enter it, we leave the daylight, moving from the bright, sun-drenched Saturday afternoons of Mississippi football crowds back into the murky evening world of fanatical sexuality we have just emerged from—of *Psychopathia Sexualis*, after all.

Since Petronius's day, at least, authors have purveyed deviate forms of sexual activity; and since Homer's, readers of proper literature have listened to the exploits of heroes. In *The Hamlet*, William Faulkner merges the two, offering a modern-day Mars not rewarded with the divine flesh of Venus's body but doomed merely to lust after it, to fill his nostrils with the pungent smell left on the wooden schoolroom bench by the buttocks of a stupid, overdeveloped village girl in her early teens. He mingles the Sick and Smiling aspects of reality in our literature. How far he has taken that literature in so doing, we are in a position to realize the better in that again a model of classic romantic fiction is offered to us by which to judge him. This time the model is not Victorian Southern, but Early American, for the first part of the Eula Varner story in *The Hamlet* is a variation on Washington Irving's "The Legend of Sleepy Hollow." This time, moreover, to compare the two stories is to respond to an invitation issued by William Faulkner himself. From this comparison we derive another awareness of the giant steps that Faulkner, with other moderns, has taken toward retrieving for readers the professional prerogatives lost at Henry Fielding's death, and particularly sexual desire (one of those "things we do and know perfectly well . . . , though we never speak of them") as a paramount motive in a young man's attentions to a young woman—sex, even the morbid forms its suppression can take.

Faulkner's story is in numerous respects a recognizable copy of Irving's, both on the literal level of plot and characterization and on a higher one. It is only because of the striking differences—which I shall stress —that we have not thought of the Eula-Labove story in this light before. The basic correspondences are immediately evident. Each hero is a young stranger who comes into the community to teach school and is attracted to the daughter of one of the most prominent natives. When, after biding his time, he summons up the courage to declare his intentions, she rebuffs him. Then he undergoes a second, more serious rebuff, this time from a man whose own affairs are closely connected with the heroine's. Whereupon he leaves abruptly and finally.

Most of the smaller details match as well. Like the Connecticut Yankee Ichabod Crane new in the community of Dutch dwellers of New York, among the Van Tassels and Van Brunts and Van Rippers, so from another county Faulkner introduces to the world of Varner and Tull and Littlejohn a stranger with the outlandish surname of Labove (the only name by which he is ever referred to). Each is thin (Crane, "exceedingly lank"; Labove, "gaunt"); ugly; with a long nose; and wearing a jacket too small for him. Each depends upon others for largesse with which to eke out his wages. The horse that Ichabod rides to his final defeat is by courtesy of his host; all through Faulkner's story Labove rides his host's horse the forty miles to and from Jefferson and wears the football coach's gift of an overcoat (even puts it on with a flourish to wear at what he thinks of as his self-immolation, the final and deadly confrontation with Jody). Each asserts his mastery in a one-room schoolhouse, maintaining order among the older boys by the use of his fists. Yet after hours each relaxes his discipline to fraternize: Ichabod associates with the older boys and plays games with them, while Labove gets a basketball court built and teaches the older boys to play the game. The Sleepy Hollow schoolhouse has windows "partly glazed, and partly patched with leaves of old copy-books"; the one in Frenchman's Bend has a window broken, with boards nailed over it temporarily.

The authority of Irving's schoolmaster is restricted to his importance "in the female circle of a rural neighborhood"; Faulkner tells us that while Labove enjoys the appellation of "professor," it is a "woman's distinction, functioning actually in a woman's world like the title of reverend." The many demands on the country schoolmaster's time include those of social occasions. Thus in addition to his teaching by day, Ichabod teaches psalmody one night a week, and meets Katrina, daughter of the wealthy farmer Van Tassel; on Friday nights, when there are parties in the Frenchman's Bend schoolhouse, Labove is of course in attendance to supervise (and to commit imaginary acts of physical assault on the center of attention on such occasions, Eula Varner, daughter of the man who runs the school). Yet each leads a characteristically male private existence. To pay for his board, Ichabod helps make hay, drives cows from pasture, and cuts firewood. To fulfill the terms of the agreement by which he works his way through the university, Labove rises in the dark to "build fires in the houses of five different faculty members and return to feed and milk." And of course, he lives for six years in a room in Frenchman's Bend that has no heat.

At last, each departs suddenly and mysteriously. In Irving's story, the boys assemble at the schoolhouse the morning after Ichabod's disaster and stroll idly about the banks of the brook, but no schoolmaster appears. His borrowed horse, the old Gunpowder, "was found without his saddle, and with the bridle under his feet, soberly cropping the grass at his master's gate." Labove leaves Frenchman's Bend on foot, but it is possible that there is an echo of Ichabod's panicked ride by night (before his further flight on foot, after being thrown) in the account given by Faulkner (in Chapter 2) of the sudden departure of

Labove's first successor in the quest for Eula's body, the traveling salesman who is mysteriously routed by her one night: "at daylight the next morning the hostler found the rented horse and buggy tied to the stable door in Jefferson and that afternoon the night station agent told of a frightened and battered man in a pair of ruined ice-cream pants who had bought a ticket on the early train." Ichabod has on his person his quarter's pay when he disappears, whereas Labove does not stop to collect his, but the inventory of each's belongings is like that of the other, even allowing for the sameness of possessions that rural bachelor school-teachers, of whatever century, may be expected to accumulate: Crane leaves a rusty razor, a few books (dreams, witchcraft), and two shirts and a half; Labove owns, in addition to the mismatched trousers and coat he wears, a razor, a few books (law, classics), and two shirts. After disappearing, Ichabod is rumored to have worked his way through law school by teaching school, "turned politician, electioneered," and so forth; Labove, whose father tells Varner that the young man wants to be governor, of course works his way through college and law school by playing football and teaching school in Frenchman's Bend. Just as there was no pressing demand for either in an agricultural society, so neither departing pedagogue is missed. The villagers in Sleepy Hollow "are apt to consider the costs of schooling a grievous burden, and schoolmasters as mere drones"; Hans Van Ripper "from that time forward determined to send his children no more to school; observing, that he never knew any good come of this same reading and writing." Since he was single and owed no money, no one thinks about Ichabod afterwards. The schoolhouse, deserted, falls into decay (another building is selected elsewhere and another teacher appears). Before Labove's appearance, and after the fiasco of his predecessor, "nobody minded especially whether the school functioned the next year or not. . . . They sent their children to it only when there was no work for them to do at home." For almost two years after Labove's disappearance (we learn in Chapter 2) the school-house is used only for community parties.

In view of the abundance of these parallels of plot, setting, and description, when Eula, successfully re-pelling Labove's advances, administers the coup de grâce of her spoken scorn, when she denounces him (Faulkner lavishing on this speech nine of the thirty-four words she speaks during the entirety of the sixty pages of a story that bears her name) with "Stop pawing me, . . . You old headless horseman Ichabod Crane," her reference to Irving's story, inaccuracy and all, seems quite to the point.

Presented, then, with the probability that Faulkner selected Irving's story as a model, or, better, as a theme on which to work his own variations (even, possibly, courting reader consciousness of what he was doing), we are enabled to explore the uses that can be made of the same materials by authors apparently as irreconcilable artistically as these two are. The story of a prodigious frog, transplanted thousands of miles and years away from Boeotia and put into the mouth of a nineteenth-century character in California, emerges with its own unique features clearly stamped upon it, for all that it draws its sustenance from an ancient and public well. Even the precise, northern European ele-gance of Bach can lend itself to the native rhythms of the Latin temperament, as Hector Villalobos has demonstrated. William Faulkner too has produced a unique effect with the old materials by bringing an old ghost story up to date and shaping it along the new, shocking, psychosexual lines of the modern literary imagination.

There are here for our scrutiny two storybook suitors, and if there are also two courted women, these serve not the cause of romance but as reflectors or registers of the thought processes of the suitors, neither of whom can, by however liberal a definition, be considered ordinary. Neither Irving's nor Faulkner's Jack sees his Jill as merely herself, with a mind and a personality and physical proportions (though in both stories these are most impressive to the male eye), but as the embodiment of something else. This something it is that he is determined to possess, not the girl herself. Neither is in love at all. One wants to take possession of a substantial farm property; the other, of a human Venusberg. The distance therefore between the two visions is ocean-wide. Whereas Labove's never descends below the level of symbol and myth, Ichabod Crane's never rises above the level of dollars. And yet, so invisibly does each author permit his hero's thoughts to shuttle between innocence and naughtiness that perhaps Faulkner's story is distinguished merely by his making verbal—albeit mythically verbal —what Irving had to leave implicit or even had to hide.

The impersonal eye looking at Eula Varner at the age of not quite thirteen takes in an incredibly large physical mass. Already "bigger than most grown women," she has breasts "no longer the little, hard fiercely pointed cones of puberty or even maidenhood." But more. Because her disdain for males is equally larger than life, Labove sees her as something more than human, as Titanic, even godlike. In terms of fact, though Jody Varner would have refused Labove his sister's hand, the match would not have been rare: mature country girls of Eula's age do marry, and marry men ten years older (not least when their fathers feel toward them the something less than paternal protectiveness that Will Varner discloses in Chapter 2 in refusing to lose his composure at the news that Eula is pregnant by an unknown man: "Hell and damnation, all this hullabaloo and uproar. . . . What did you expect—that she would spend the rest of her life just running water through it?") But if, in the obsession that gradually overruns Labove's thoughts about her, he soon gives up the idea of ever marrying Eula, it is not because he retains to this extent his reason but because he never considers the possibility of any mortal man aspiring to husbandhood with the inexhaustible fertility that her body symbolizes. How, after all, does an earthborn propose to Ceres? "He saw it: the fine land rich and fecund and foul and eternal and impervious to him who claimed title to it, oblivious, drawing to itself tenfold the quantity of living seed its owner's whole life could have secreted and compounded, producing a thousandfold the harvest he could ever hope to gather and save."

Crane's vision also takes in a sexually mature specimen of young womanhood (of a more proper age, eighteen); Irving allows himself merely the liberty of saying that Katrina is "blooming" and "plump." Possibly Faulkner's reference (in Chapter 2) to "the ripe peach which [Eula's] full damp mouth resembled" is a surrealistic variation on Irving's formula simile for Katrina, presented as "as . . . ripe . . . as one of her father's peaches." (A generation later Thackeray would proceed no further—and he, unlike Irving, had need to—burying as he does that fleeting reference to "the famous frontal development" of Rebecca Sharp in his vast epic, and giving the phrase to a physician, for double safety.) Yet the object by which Irving conjures up for Ichabod the vision of his lady fair is the sumptuous Van Tassel farmhouse, and the fair demesnes that there adjacent lie. Ichabod too sees his love not in person but as what she (and, with luck, he) will one day inherit; and curiously his vision seems to be the original and simple one which Faulkner raised to the symbolic dimension of Labove's, just quoted. Ichabod earlier, as "he rolled his great green eyes over the fat meadowlands," had also seen "the fine land rich and fecund" of Labove's vision in "the rich fields of wheat, of rye, of buckwheat, and Indian corn, and the orchards burthened with ruddy fruit" of the Van Tassel farm; but his was a shorter flight of the imagination, for "his heart yearned after the damsel who was to inherit these domains, and his imagination expanded with the idea, how they might be readily turned into cash."

Inasmuch as Ichabod's thoughts are domestically oriented, they naturally stray, even if unconsciously, to the physical intimacy of married couples. In fact, it is in just such domestic terms that he thinks of the Van Tassel menagerie. His "devouring mind's eye" sees the pigeons "snugly put to bed" and the ducks "pairing cosily in dishes, like snug married couples." Eventually (in what is at the same time the most innocent and the bawdiest of such mental images), he beholds the yellow pumpkins "turning their fair round bellies to the sun" and giving "ample prospects" of great issue. In Irving's story, the "prospects had to be as normal as pumpkin pie, precisely. But what other prospects might be suggested by this chaste yet insinuating metaphor, we can find in Faulkner's variation. It is as though he too had wondered what might result from so evidently ample a pregnancy, for he gives to the coarsely humorous account by Eula's father (much later in *The Hamlet*) of the conception of the Gargantuan Eula herself the very words of Irving's metaphor (filtered, possibly, through the style of Sut Luvingood),

> ". . . there was a old woman told my mammy once that if a woman showed her belly to the full moon after

she had done caught, it would be a gal. So Mrs. Varner taken and laid every night with the moon on her nekid belly, until it fulled and after. . . . You might try it. You get enough women showing their nekid bellies to the moon or the sun either or even just to your hand fumbling around often enough and more than likely after a while there will be something in it you can lay your ear and listen to, provided something come up and you aint got away by that time."

The "winter squashes," on the other hand, of a writer (Hawthorne) whose influence on Faulkner is demonstrable, are presented in "The Old Manse" far more circumspectly, not only as to language but as to sex, lying as they do "strewn upon the soil, big, round fellows, hiding their heads beneath the leaves, but turning their great yellow rotundities to the noontide sun."

In other little ways the twentieth-century hero's vision seems a deliberate variation on Irving's. It was noted above, for example, that both Crane and Labove have a long nose. Actually, Irving tells us that Crane's is a "long snipe nose . . . that . . . looked like a weathercock," and he does so to sound his first comic pitch, for not only does Crane look ludicrous but, thinking like a fool too, he is capable of infinite self-deception. Confident of winning Katrina, he treats himself to expansive visions of the prosperity and felicity that are to ensue. His "busy" fancy presents to him "the blooming Katrina, with a whole family of children, mounted on the top of a wagon loaded with household trumpery, with pots and kettles dangling beneath; and he beheld himself bestriding a pacing mare, with a colt at her heels, setting forth for . . . the Lord knows where." And later, at the quilting frolic at the end of which he proposes to Katrina and is rejected, as he gorges himself on food "he could not help rolling his large eyes round him . . . and chuckling with the possibility that he might one day be lord of all this scene of almost unimaginable luxury and splendor." On the other hand, Labove's is the "long nose of thought." He is quite aware that he is mad and sick, and senses that his quest for Eula is doomed, with a self-knowledge that is clairvoyant. Something is going to happen, he knows, and "he knew too that, whatever it would be, he would be the vanquished, even though he did not know yet what the one crack in his armor was and that she would find it unerringly and instinctively and without ever being aware that she had been in deadly danger." Thus, when he gravely approaches what he thinks will be the fatal duel with the brother of the girl he thinks he has gravely affronted, a cheap commercial advertisement on the door to Varner's store seems to him to mock his vanquished self with the very success and affluence that his unflinching self-analysis has always told him will never be his. What his keen mind sees at this climactic moment, as he looks at the advertisement, is Ichabod Crane's fancied family picture but distorted and refracted by his mercilessly analytical state of mind: "the reproduction of a portrait, smug, bearded, successful, living far away and married, with children, in a rich house and beyond the reach of passion and blood's betrayal."

The intensity of that last phrase is congruous with the character that Faulkner has given to his hero; and whereas Irving also lets the light of imagination play over his characters, it is for quite a different purpose. Irving's is a comic story about a skinny schoolmaster with fat dreams of winning an heiress, "an odd mixture of small shrewdness and simple credulity," with a superstitious and unmanly dread of ghosts; it relies for its effects on suspense (as to whether the crane-like

Ichabod will win the fat Dutch girl and then, whether the headless horseman will ride that night); it is, therefore, while incidentally grim, prevailingly humorous. Conversely, Faulkner's gaunt schoolmaster is an intense, passionate, fierce (knocking football opponents unconscious without being aware of it), principled man impelled irrationally toward a downfall that he senses from the start; its greatest effect is its shockingly intimate exposition of the workings of the doomed man's mind; thus, while incidentally humorous, it is prevailingly grim; self-exposure and mortification of one's pride create a havoc in Faulkner's striver after success and mastery immeasurably greater than the power of any ghost.

This being so, Irving's metaphor strives for mock-epic effects, while Faulkner's, for nothing short of epic itself. By power of quotation and allusion, Sleepy Hollow acquires an atmosphere of Elsinore and the storm-racked heath before Dover; the characterization of the loutish yokel Brom Bones is in terms of the *Iliad*; and Ichabod himself is swathed in Miltonic reference. Irving's imagination extends even to hagiology, as when Ichabod is likened to St. Vitus. But his is a comic saint, for it is Vitus as patron of the dance. Faulkner too deals in hagiology, but to prepare his readers for the violent action Labove will eventually resort to. His face a thousand years ago would, Faulkner tells us, "have been a monk's, a militant fanatic who would have turned his uncompromising back upon the world with actual joy and gone to a desert and passed the rest of his days and nights calmly . . . battling . . . with his own fierce and unappeasable natural appetites." At another time, as Faulkner limns him, he has "the hungry mouth, the insufferable humorless eyes, the intense ugly blue-shaved face like a composite photograph of Voltaire and an Elizabethan pirate." What wonder, then, that he sees Eula not merely as an abnormally large and well-developed country girl but as Venus, as "out of the old Dionysic times"; as the uterus personified, or "the drowsing maidenhead symbol's self"; as having "that ungirdled quality of the very goddesses" in the Homer and Thucydides he has been reading; or, when she is eating her lunch, as "one of the unchaste and perhaps even anonymously pregnant immortals eating bread of Paradise on a sunwise slope of Olympus." (Later in the volume, Faulkner in his own person associates her with Venus, with Brunhilde.) Ichabod's is an imagination incapable of ever seeing a goddess go; but then, as might be expected of a ghost story, Katrina is given three or four lines of characterization and description during its entirety.

Now it is also true that the goddess whom Labove watches at her lunch eats only one dish, and that is not bread of Paradise but cold baked sweet potatoes; and if her leather school-satchel never contains any other object, this is Faulkner's way of presenting the torpidity, the emptiness of the tiny cranial cavity that presides over the mountain of flesh that is her body. To think of her, then, in mythic terms, as Labove does, is comic; if it is not dangerously less than this— that is to say, silly—it is that it is due to the madness that rules his thinking about and visualizations of Eula and even more important, that it is a self-conscious madness, as we have seen. (Like the tall convict in *The Wild Palms*, Labove has been "betrayed" by his reading matter: he imagines Eula's husband-to-be in Homeric terms, as a "crippled Vulcan to that Venus." And during his last three years of sexual torture in Frenchman's Bend, he sees the "bleak schoolhouse, the little barren village" as "his Gethsemane and . . . his Golgotha too.") This explains the comedy of the scene in Jefferson when Labove's landlady offers her Spartan, ascetic roomer the "treat" of a single baked sweet potato, then cries, "Why, Mr. Labove, you are sick!" While comic in still another, much lower, sense is the view through Will Varner's eyes of the dress of the Labove family. Here is a ten-year-old girl with a tattered but clean gingham dress on her shoulders, and on her feet—a pair of football shoes, man-sized and cleated. Here is an ancient woman wearing on Sundays, summer and winter, a heavy dark blue sweater with a big red varsity "M" on it, the sweater "sprawled . . . across her shrunken chest and stomach as she sat in her chair and rocked and sucked the dead little pipe"—she too wearing a man's cleated football shoes. If Irving's metaphors suggest the playful travesty of epic such as we find in Fielding, then certainly Faulkner's scene of the young rural god, sick with lust for the distant baked-sweet-potato-eating goddess, being offered a baked sweet potato is to be thought of as a travesty of, say, the mourning country doctor Charles Bovary finding in a drawer the bundle of love letters that Emma had received from someone else. While for Faulkner's grotesquely shod farm family, we must go to the hillbillies of caricature that were appearing in *Esquire* magazine cartoons at the time Faulkner wrote *The Hamlet*. Grandmother Labove, or course, still lives on, transformed into the vulgar Loweezy of the *Snuffy Smith* cartoon strip. Yet the Labove story is actually not a funny story at all.

Yet it is remarkable that two stories so different in tone and in intention proceed to their conclusions in a manner that, structurally speaking, is practically identical. Both storytellers plot the downward course of their hero's fortunes in two stages. In both stories, the first stage is a man-woman confrontation, while the second, which follows immediately, is man-to-man. In "The Legend of Sleepy Hollow" Ichabod Crane's last day in the village leads to two unfortunate developments. First, his personal suit is rejected by Katrina; then he is utterly banished (by fright) by Brom Bones, another suitor. In *The Hamlet* Labove's personal suit is rejected by Eula; then he is utterly banished (by mortification) by Jody, her brother. Both authors stage their scene so that first the hero and heroine can be alone, and that the hero's first setback can in turn set the stage for his second, which is the real rout. But what a striking departure is Faulkner's! He has told us that the two halves of *The Wild Palms* are opposite versions of the same theme, that the convict story is merely an inside-out version of the Charlotte-Harry story. Now it is as though he had decided to turn Irving's story inside out, to burlesque it. The technique he uses is bathos.

Since "The Legend of Sleepy Hollow" is not a love story, Irving plays down the first stage of Crane's disaster; dismisses it, in fact, summarily, declining to divulge what was said during Ichabod's "tête-à-tête" with Katrina: "What passed at this interview I will not pretend to say, for in fact I do not know." This pretense of ignorance stems, of course, not from his unwillingness or inability to attempt the dialogue of courtship but from the fact that what happens during the interview is as nothing compared to what is about to happen. To that, as we shall see, he bends his efforts mightily.

So far from skirting the scene between his schoolmaster and his plump heroine, Faulkner leads up to it dramatically and then develops it into one of the most amazing demonstrations of courtship in American literature. From innocent tête-à-tête we go now to an earnest attempt by a law-school graduate at the criminal assault of a girl barely in her teens. And for an understanding of what passed at this interview the reader must bring to these pages a knowledge not of Ichabod Crane's ancient treatises on witchcraft but of the modern ones of Masoche, de Sade, and Kraft-Ebing. To prepare us for the violence that is to be released in the schoolhouse, Faulkner tells us of the thoughts that have been usurping the customary ones in Labove's mind during the past few years. We learn that he has been alternating between wanting "to hurt her, see blood spring and run, watch that serene face warp to the indelible mark of terror and agony beneath his own" and wanting to abase himself before this girl, to "grovel in the dust" before her, panting: "Show me what to do. Tell me. I will do anything you tell me." He has also, for some time now, taken to "wallowing his face" on her place on the schoolroom bench, still warm from her buttocks and still smelling of her. Returning for her satchel now after the close of school, she catches him in this act and he attacks her.

When had serious literature shown a lover in a state of greater undress than Labove, face to the bench, nostrils drinking in the odor of the body of this stupid mass of flesh? The course of modern realism in art extends all the way back to Brueghel; and in literature, at least back to Cervantes; yet who had dared as much as this—who except outside literature, in psychiatry, or below it, in pornography? In Thackeray's own day, to be sure, Walt Whitman had claimed for himself the place of spokesman for the "many long dumb voices," including those "of the diseased and despairing."

Through me forbidden voices,
Voices of sexes and lusts . . . voices veiled, and I
    remove the veil . . . .

Yet at once these "voices indecent" become "clarified and transfigured" by the poet, who speaks of his function in religious terms. All things human are divine, Whitman insists, "and I make holy whatever I touch or am touched from." The same vatic treatment invests a sexual scene in Sherwood Anderson's *Winesburg, Ohio*: "The Strength of God" is about a minister who faintly suggests Faulkner's desperately possessed, fanatical schoolmaster enduring a cold room for six years while awaiting his opportunity to make himself known to a female whose body he lusts after. The Reverend Curtis Hartman takes to watching a shapely schoolmistress in bed next door from the church-tower room where he prepares his sermons; finally, one cold winter night he comes out and sits in the tower room, his feet wet, and after shivering in the cold, finally bloodies his fist from knocking out with it the leaded glass window that obstructs his complete view of the naked woman. But again the religious significance ascribed to the episode gives it a dimension of transcendance: the pane that the Reverend Hartman smashes is a scene of Christ and a child, and the very act of smashing it—of destroying, that is, his lust—has had a redemptive effect on him, as he announces, "The strength of God was in me and I broke it with my fist." This is at any rate the intensity of Faulkner's Labove. And certainly we can find it in Eugene O'Neill plays (*Desire Under the Elms* comes to mind, with its seduction and incest). But for precedents of Labove's means of sexual gratification during the late afternoons in a deserted Mississippi schoolhouse, of his wanting to hurt the girl physically or to submit himself, on his hands and knees, to whatever she might want him to do—for variations from traditional sexual behavior to equal these we must go to the literature of Europe. To Ned Ward's *London Spy*, where the visitor to England is treated to the strange sight of an elderly man inquiring of a brothel mistress whether a new shipment of iron rods has yet arrived. Or to Proust's novel, when the narrator, curious about cries coming from inside the door of a room in the hotel where he has taken refuge during a Zeppelin raid in Paris peers over the transom to discover that they are being made by the Baron de Charlus, who is complaining that the boy beating him is betraying his lack of love by the perfunctoriness of his beating. Finally, to where all such literary examples deserve treatment—to the clinic of Richard von Krafft-Ebing. Here we can find sadism formally considered as "Injury to Woman": ". . . injury of the victim of lust and sight of the victim's blood are a delight and pleasure." Here, too, we can find: "MASOCHISM. THE ASSOCIATION OF PASSIVELY ENDURED CRUELTY AND VIOLENCE WITH LUST." "For the masochist the principal thing is subjection to the woman. . . . For him the act . . . is a means to the end of mental satisfaction of his peculiar desires." [10]

The second and final act of Irving's play is vintage Gothic. Departing late at night from the Van Tassel home, the superstitious Ichabod, now "heavy-hearted and crest-fallen" from his rejection by Katrina, is slowly, carefully, and excitingly converted from mere dejection into suspicion, then fear, and finally into a panicked human being galloping madly over a country road at midnight with an intolerably horrible apparition in closer and closer pursuit until, when last seen, he has been struck from behind by a horrible missile, thrown from his horse, and "tumbled headlong into the dust." The order of events during these last hours of Irving's story is classically climactic.

Faulkner's second half does the same, for all that in

the last moments reader and victim alike are over-whelmed, not by climax, but by an anticlimax that crushes Labove as devastatingly as the pumpkin routed Crane. Eula does not so much reject Labove as send him sprawling, and emerges from his quick and ruthless grasping and groping affected almost not at all. "Breathing deep but not panting and not even dishevelled," she leaves the schoolhouse, returns merely for her satchel (forgotten this second time), gets it and leaves for good. It is from the point of her second return to the end of the story an hour or so later, that Labove's proper terror begins and mounts, moment by moment, as intolerably as Ichabod's. He had, of course, never expected his attempt to possess Eula's body to succeed. Now, rising to his feet and to the bravery that he feels the occasion demands, he prepares himself for the real ordeal: the duel to the death with Jody, her brother, who will demand satis-faction for the crude insult offered to his younger sister. (A shadowy adversary of sorts, like Ichabod's Brom Bones, Jody has—at least, Labove wildly sur-mises—endured "five years of violent and unsupported conviction" that Labove would do what he has just attempted.) Every moment now is an ominous noise or silence in the solitude of a deserted schoolhouse in late afternoon that is as thronging with threats to his body as are the night woods above Tarry Town that the dejected Ichabod must traverse on his way home from Katrina's. The first time the tinny ticking of the cheap clock is interrupted by the opening of the door, it is not the avenger, after all, who enters but the girl herself, and returning merely for her satchel; and here we are to contemplate the exquisite irony of a highly intelligent but now unbearably shamed man watching the return to the scene of his humiliation of his victo-rious adversary not to reopen the to-him vitally important physical relationship but to recover an object of infinitely greater concern to her primitive intelligence than his designs on her body—namely, the leather container for her sweet potatoes. This crisis, in turn, now past, Labove simultaneously welcomes and dreads the inevitable appearance of Jody, anticipating the battle with a riot of sexual metaphor and rage: better the penetration of Jody's body (with Labove's fists) than no penetration of a Varner at all; would this not be "an orgasm of sorts"—even (here his traitorous books have him shift from Homer to Aristotle) a *katharsis?*

Preparing for the confrontation with as deliberate a ceremony as that with which a criminal accused of a capital crime is asked to rise to hear the verdict of the returning jury, Labove goes to his desk, squares the clock face toward him in order the better to be able to time Jody's appearance in terms of "horse distance"; surveys the space available for the battle when it shall formally begin, as begin it must; considers awaiting the onslaught outside; and waits. After the unnerving ticking has lasted for an hour and no avenger has appeared, he decides that his adversary is waiting for him to make the advance. Gravely he arranges his personal affairs in the schoolroom, then emerging into the fateful daylight he starts toward the Varner store, where he is sure Jody is waiting for him. With "his face tragic and calm now, walking on down toward the store," where many surely will witness his defeat and death by gunfire, Labove is (and so would seem to himself if his reading had included Zane Grey as well as Homer) menaced by the daylight apparition of public defeat. But when the inside of the store is as vacant of witnesses as the outside, his bafflement and anxiety become unbearable. Then, an eternity (of seconds) later, he discovers that Jody has no interest whatsoever in Labove's presence before him. But this realization, stunning as it is, is as nothing compared with the other to which it inevitably leads: Jody simply doesn't know, because Eula has not even bothered to tell him about the attack. "She never told him at all. She didn't even forget to. She doesn't even know anything happened that was worth mentioning." After all, it had been merely the bursting down of the dam of his restraint by the torrent of his years of longing and self-torture.

It is with this realization, this anticlimax, that Faulkner destroys Labove as thoroughly as Irving's headless horseman had vanquished Ichabod Crane a century before near a country churchyard at the witching time of night. Labove walks straight out of Frenchman's Bend without bothering to claim his meager personal belongings and is never heard of again. And if it is difficult for us even now to accept as one of the realities of this life his violence of thought (yet we accept his forbears in the *Inferno*), the thwarted and misdirected force of his sexuality, how much more difficult is it for us to believe that so extravagant a plant grew from so inauspicious a seed.

7

J. D. Salinger

"De Daumier-Smith's Blue Period" is a phase in the young life of the painter-teacher who tells the story. It is one that he enters and from which he emerges toward the end of the story. Our concern is with the reason why the Blue Period began, then why it ended; with the factors or events causing it and then those which are responsible for his outgrowing it. Here we become aware of a variety of correspondences to Salinger's story, two of which are important to our understanding of it: one of these is from German poetry and the other, from French painting. Even with this awareness, the full intent of "De Daumier-Smith's Blue Period" may evade us, its underlying sentiment being carefully restrained—even mocked good-naturedly—perhaps in an attempt to avoid mawkishness. And understandably, if so. For what Salinger has written is an intimate confession of the irrational conduct that grief at his mother's death caused in a young man of nineteen in the year 1939.

The story opens with the removal, resulting from her death, of her son and her husband (but the son's stepfather) from Paris back to New York. The young man (his name is probably John Smith, but we are never told) reacts by rejecting both New York and stepfather. He chafes at the enforced intimacy of the room they share at the Ritz, at his dependence on the stepfather for everything. His other rejection takes the form of revulsion at the crudity and commercialism of the culture of his new home, New York City (in which he spent the first ten years of his life), and a steadfast devotion to the charm of the old one, France. This latter brings about an early departure from both stepfather and step-country. Off the young man goes to the only French civilization he is in a position to afford, Montreal. The term by which, years later, he describes his mental condition at this point in his life is applied indirectly, but it is borrowed directly from psychiatry: it is trauma.

He has been accepted as an instructor in a correspondence school of art in Montreal run by a Japanese couple for students that none of them ever see. This provides a complete suspension of reality for young Smith, who has arrived affecting a completely new identity (dress, name, age, and so on) and who has chosen this way of living as necessary to sustain his illusion. (What other measures he takes we shall see shortly.)

At first, disillusion threatens. The Yoshotos treat him with mysterious impersonality; his quarters border on primitiveness; and they give him no work to do worthy of his talents. Then, as he is accepted and given pupils of his own, he recovers his peace of mind. Even the ineptitude of his first pupils does not dismay him, for among them is one, Sister Irma, whose work, untutored though it is, reveals a talent that excites him. He pours out professional advice (and makes personal advances) to her in his letter. But this dear relationship with the correspondence student is abruptly ended by a note from the father superior canceling her enrollment in the course.

Before and after this setback, he has a most unusual experience. This is the crisis toward which his frame of mind has been impelling him. When it is over, the story ends quickly. What happens is that he has a vision: first, a foreshadowing, then a veritable initiation. Both occur in front of the window of an orthopedics appliance store, above which the art institute has its quarters. Although he both does and does not invest this vision with the importance of an epiphany or religious revelation, that is actually what it is, incongruity, comedy, and all.

In the experience that foreshadows his initiation, a "hideous" intuition visits him while he is still in a state of excitement and expectation about the reply awaited from Sister Irma. He looks at the display in the window and thinks that "no matter how coolly or sensibly or gracefully I might one day learn to live my life, I would always at best be a visitor in a garden of enamel urinals and bedpans, with a sightless, wooden dummy-deity standing by in a marked-down rupture-truss."

As for the vision itself that comes later, his commentary on it both deprecates and aggrandizes it. Disclaimer and all, he devotes a fairly substantial paragraph entirely to preparing the reader for it. While not "even a border-line case . . . of genuine mysticism," still it is "extremely out of the way," is "extraordinary," and "quite transcendent." This time he actually sees a visitor in the garden of enamel urinals and bedpans, tending the wooden dummy. His presence and friendly gesture discompose the young woman. She falls, but then recovers and resumes her work. At this point, the young man experiences a blinding sensation that dizzies him. When he can see again, the girl is gone and the vision is over, but not its effects.

This much of the story we perceive, however indistinctly, by ourselves. But the crucial vision that brings about this change of affairs will continue to seem unaccountably incongruous in its seriousness, even intensity, in a story characteristically self-mocking, even comical, if we do not recognize it for what it appears to be: a burlesque, possibly even of two famous visions, one ancient, the other modern, and both intensely religious.

The one of the visions which Salinger draws upon is from the New Testament, and I shall discuss it separately below. The other seems to be that of the poet Rainer Maria Rilke in the museum. In fact, understanding of "De Daumier-Smith's Blue Period" may not be possible unless we collate it with Rilke's widely known poem "Archäischer Torso Apollos." In the columns below, the correspondences between poem and story are set opposite each other.

Rilke	Salinger
The torso is on display in a museum. It is of Apollo, god of manly beauty; thus, a model of physical perfection.	The model of a male torso is on display in a shop-window. Such models are usually of perfect proportions, in terms of their purpose. A minion (window dresser) attends it.
The torso is disfigured, lacking head and, presumably, lower legs and feet.	The model is "sightless" and, more important, is a "dummy-*deity*" (my italics). He is disfigured (ruptured).
Apollo's missing head is imagined in garden terms, as the place wherein "the eye-apples ripened."	Our last view of the shop-window dominated by the "deity" is of "a shimmering field of . . . flowers"; our first, of a "garden."
From the slight twist of the torso's loins a smile goes toward its genitals.	From the narrator's eyes a smile goes toward the woman tending the model's genitals.

The torso seems to be lighted up: it glows and gleams as though in the light of a candelabrum, turned off now but still gleaming.

The narrator views the sightless model from the darkness. The first time "it was after dark" when he "looked into the lighted display-window"; the second, "In the nine o'clock twilight, as I approached, . . . , there was a light on. . . ." The "field of . . . enamel flowers" is a "shimmering" one.

The one great impression that Apollo gives is of a god whose eyes impress the more for their absence: they gleam, blind (via the chest), glint, and break out like a star.

The sun strikes the narrator with immeasurable swiftness and blinds him. He has to back away from the window (he who has said of himself, "I am willing to stay in the dark") and can't bear to look back at it.

This impression is so great that the viewer cannot remain the same afterwards. He must become another person: he must change his life, presumably for a truer, more honest one / in such a piercing gaze / .

De Daumier-Smith cannot remain the same. He leaves off his designs on Sister Irma and reinstates the students he has expelled. (His letters for this purpose "seemed to write themselves.") He leaves Montreal, goes back to the United States, and completely gives up his false identity.

You must change your life, Rilke insists. Change his life Salinger's hero does, and immediately. He renounces his pose, his Blue Period. (The post-epiphany entry in his diary is still in French, to be sure; but the letters that he writes after that are, for the first time, written from a chair, instead of the Blue Period cushions on the floor.) He, who had scorned his step-father for his carnality (the proper young blonde divorcee with him that day, De Daumier-Smith's willful mental deviltry had accused of being a "wanton" and her eyes of sparkling with "depravity") is leaving Sister Irma free to follow her destiny—of chastity. He, in turn, is admitting to his own carnality. As witness his frank devotion now to women's bodies in shorts on the beach. (The fact that he has to leave Montreal only a few days later because of the closing of the school is, as he tells us, merely an anticlimactic sequel to his vision.)

If we grant that Salinger's hero's vision is a burlesque refraction of Rilke's solemn original, we want to know what prompted him to encourage us to establish the connection, however concealed. In order to answer this, we must at least try to unravel the mystery of the vision in the window.

Who is the young woman there? Possibly the hero identifies her with the Sister Irma he has never seen, but possibly with himself. The latter we might suspect from his tendency to see himself everywhere: all during the return voyage to the United States "I used our stateroom mirror to note my uncanny physical resemblance to El Greco" and during the stay, after that, in New York City, when in one month he completed eighteen oil paintings, "noteworthily enough," he tells us, "seventeen . . . were self-portraits." The story's many details, moreover, invite this interpretation. The ages, for example, identify the two as one and the same. The girl is "about thirty," the age that he himself had falsely given in his lie-crammed letter of application to Yoshoto. The colors of the young woman's dress are equally significant. Dressed as she is in green, yellow, and lavender chiffon, she is as ostentatiously vulgar as he in the clothing he had put on for his arrival in Montreal and meeting with the head of an art school: beige gaberdine suit, navy-blue shirt, yellow tie, brown-and-white shoes, yellow (Panama) hat, and a reddish-brown moustache grown for the occasion. He notes that she is "hefty," suggesting a carnality which surely he recognizes in his feelings toward (surely not in his visualization of) Sister Irma.

Other possibilities grow out of the identification proposed above. In his first, preparatory, intuition arising from his gazing into the window, he had foreseen himself as a visitor in such a garden as this; is he not—albeit in the form of this young woman—precisely the visitor now? As he looks at her, she is in the act of tending a god of beauty; he too, as art teacher, had been tending an art god. And so intimately! For the young woman "changing the truss on the wooden dummy" is being observed by the young man who had spent part of an afternoon "doing overlay corrections on some male and female nudes (sans sex organs) that R. Howard Ridgefield had genteelly and obscenely drawn." Finally, when seen in the embarrassing wantonness—as it were—of her actions, she is so covered with shame that she blushes and loses her balance; when he sees himself in this light, he undergoes a blinding sensation that confirms the first vision he had had, earlier. The final parallel between young woman in the window and young man watching her is beyond doubt the most curious of all. While living in New York City after his return from France, the ill-at-ease young expatriate had had a disagreeable experience in a crowded bus. Standing "buttocks to buttocks" with the man behind him in a crowded bus, he had disregarded the driver's request that standees move back until the driver had turned toward him and ordered him to "move" his "ass." This incident, the young man tells us, was significant. Why? we may have wondered. He does not tell us, but we may suppose that now, looking into the Montreal shop window, he sees himself in this young woman who falls and lands heavily on her bottom. In so doing, she moves her ass, just as he had finally done in New York City. Perhaps this is why, in reaching out toward the hefty blonde and hitting only the glass, he is to be thought of as trying to reach out toward himself and not succeeding.

You must, Rilke tells the looker-on in the museum, react drastically to this torso. There is not a place on it that does not see you. From this blinding total scrutiny nothing less than a complete alteration can result in you. Your life can never be the same. You are under as forcible a compulsion to change it as compels the Ancient Mariner's storytelling. Salinger's hero complies, unquestioningly.

In asking the initiates among his readers to recognize the connection between his own blinding vision and that of the viewer in the Rilke poem, Salinger's young man is doing two things opposed and complementary, and consistent with the technique of self-deception and cold detachment used concomitantly throughout the story. The bus driver, for example, had been quite courteous and long-suffering before forced to resort to vulgarity, as the young man admits; he also knew that the blonde consort of his mourning stepfather in the New York City restaurant was, for all the wantonness De Daumier-Smith insisted on reading into her every word and glance, quite a chaste young woman. So now, for a ruptured storewindow dummy brightly lighted in a window to evoke the same response in him as that of the headless and legless torso of the manly Greek god is to burlesque his vision—a vision that is greater than Rilke's and yet for ever so much less a provocation. Yet Salinger is also achieving the opposite effect: in even proposing the parallel, he is enhancing, is magnifying the importance of the entire situation of his young man.

For the situation of this young man was, we perceive, only apparently droll. Notwithstanding the self-conscious clowning and the defensive amusement at his own morbid condition, he took it with great seriousness then, and now, ten years later, looks back upon it as such. How better, then, could he reinforce his own now mature recollection of his moping melancholy mad self as it underwent conversion in 1939 than by reaching for a magnificent parallel?

I have treated the greater part of Salinger's story above hurriedly, in order the better to emphasize the initiation scene which causes the hero to change his life. Now I should like to go back and examine that life in detail, and to propose that in order to understand the young man's exceedingly odd behavior, we must consult the facts of certain other works of art and life stories. Again we shall find echoes or allusions; again we shall wonder that they are there.

First, the hero's name. We are invited to suppose that the young narrator either has a nondescript family name or that it is actually as ignominious as the one (John Smith) that he works so odd a variation on in creating a new identity for himself. That he should assume a family relationship to the late French caricaturist, Honoré Daumier, is understandable: after all, an art lover and painter would so respond. But that he seized upon Daumier in particular involves an aptness of mimicry not immediately understood: it was Daumier who, though born in a provincial city (for Marseilles, substitute New York), moved with his family to Paris in his boyhood and grew up there. (The adventures of "The Laughing Man" take him across "the Chinese border into France, where he enjoyed flaunting his high but modest genius in the face of Marcel Dufarge, the internationally famous detective and witty consumptive," Salinger's narrator recalls. Here, of course, the playfully outrageous geography is obvious; but only the alert reader will recognize the telescoping of two Parisian names from the narrator's boyhood reading to create the equally erroneous "Dufarge": the famous detective of Poe's, *Du*pin, and the sinister knitter of Dickens's, Madame De*farge*.)

In any event, the fact of his changing his name introduces another and less recondite correspondence in the story: between Jean de Daumier-Smith (born John Smith?) and Pablo Picasso (born Pablo Ruiz P.). And since this is a most important correspondence, it is fortunate that the narrator has provided the major helps. As the young man truthlessly says, in his letter of application for the art-school instructorship, Picasso was "one of the oldest and dearest friends" of his parents. He makes Picasso the subject of his conversation with Yoshoto when they meet and even invents an anecdote that installs him, a man forty years Picasso's junior, on a level of intimacy with the great painter. Part of the absurdity needs to be examined closely: "I recalled . . . how many times I had said to him, '*M. Picasso, ou allez vous?*' and how, in response to this all-penetrating question, the master had never failed to walk slowly, leadenly, across his studio to look at a small reproduction of his *Les Saltimbanques* and the glory, long forfeited, that had been his." From so direct a hint as this, we see why De Daumier-Smith has chosen Picasso for his imaginary confidant. It is not the one he misleadingly gives us (that Picasso "seemed to me the French painter who was best known in America") but that because of his own recent and painful personal grief, he has actually begun to identify himself with Picasso. For if, as he tells us, Picasso's fame was this great in 1939, then certainly as well known were the facts of his Blue Period, whose high point was the very painting that De Daumier-Smith has just been reminiscing about. At the age of nineteen, a sudden and crushing sorrow (the death of a close friend) had caused a striking change in Picasso's life and work. One of the first signs of this was a large burial scene he painted to commemorate the man's death. This was the ushering-in of a period of melancholy, sadness, and despair —of, in the vernacular, blues—that caused him to forsake his liveliness of scene and vividness of portraiture and to substitute for them, among other subjects, "the succession of played-out prostitutes and mothers who introduce the 'blue period'"—whose paintings remain today, fifty years later, precisely what the Salinger narrator has in effect been reminding Picasso—"the most popular work of any period," as William S. Lieberman puts it.

With these facts in hand, we can perceive the meanings of various facts of the Salinger story, both those related and those now to be introduced. At the age of nineteen, its hero has been upset by his mother's death. He compares the effect of moving to Paris with the moving back to New York as follows: "Being a cool, not to say an ice-cold, ten at the time, I took the big move, so far as I know, untraumatically. It was the move back to New York, nine years later, three months after my mother died, that threw me, and threw me terribly." But eventually we see that the emphasis in the latter statement is misplaced: it was the death, more than the moving to New York, that so affected his reason. He says that both stepfather and himself "gradually discovered that we were both in love with the same deceased woman." In Montreal, tense because of the Yoshotos' seeming awareness of his disguise, he is at the point of crying out to them: "My mother's dead, and I have to live with her charming husband, and nobody in New York speaks French." And he confides to Sister Irma, by letter, that the happiest day of his life was when he was seventeen and on his way to meet his mother. As for the present, we would already have guessed from his conduct that he is trying valiantly to pretend that his mother is still alive and that he is still living in Paris, if he did not practically disclose this himself. As he confides to Sister Irma, ". . . I do not wilfully invite any unnecessary disillusions at this point in my life. I am willing to stay in the dark."

Being an art enthusiast, he naturally finds himself drawn to and identifying himself with the greatest period of Picasso's life, the Blue Period ("the glory, long forfeited, that had been his"). He develops a passion for blue. The suit which he puts on for the opening day of the art school is blue: he thinks the color "appropriate for an instructor" of art. Of all the many water colors of Yoshoto the one he still dreams of today is an exciting tour de force of blue: "white geese flying through an extremely pale-blue sky, with . . . the blueness of the sky, or an ethos of the blueness of the sky, reflected in the bird's feathers." (This impression is precisely like the one the faded autumn blossoms have on Rilke in "Blue Hydrangeas": they have no blue of their own, but reflect and mirror the blue of the sky.) He is struck by the contents of the nun's envelope, by one painting in particular. Where Picasso had first displayed his grief by painting a large burial scene of his friend Casagemas, the suicide, Sister Irma had painted a large burial scene of Christ. Equally important is a detail in this painting that the young man cites three times, a detail straight out of Picasso's famous Blue Period: a prostitute, Mary Magdalene, and a prostitute, moreover, dressed in a "blue outfit." In all of this, I think, the young man recognizes not only Picasso but himself: another possibly young person crushed by the crass burdens of daily existence (Sister Irma spends her convent life teaching cooking, as well as drawing, and to children, at that) and finding release for her spirit by expressing herself in funerals, prostitutes, and blue. She and he even have both been oppressed by a man with the same name: just as a Zimmerman was the dentist who had pulled eight of the disguised-name young instructor's teeth, so a Zimmerman was the Father who directed the life of a woman of concealed age and appearance and of real talent. This would explain why he is excited by her work and alternates technical advice with questions about her life and proposals for a meeting. These latter concerns betray his inner motives (as he eventually realizes): mixed with his dispassionate and professional attitude is a distinctly erotic one, which he as much as tells us in his well-related love fantasy. Thus, his discomfiture when he reads Father Zimmerman's letter canceling Sister Irma's enrollment, and his rediscovery of himself, made possible by the blinding experience before the shopwindow, discussed above.

As a result, he knows that his actions since returning from France have all been a madness arising from unbearable grief. Invited or not, disillusions knock at our door, and we cannot stay in the dark. Although he had tried to spiritualize his intentions toward the nun (by visualizing himself as "the Peter Abelard-type man"), his intentions all along had been erotic. So now he renounces them and demonstrates his renunciation of hypocrisy as well by giving himself over freely to the vulgar pastime of contemplating girls in shorts on the beach. "It was Freud who defined neurosis as 'abnormal attachment to the past' and who urged what Philip Rieff calls an 'ideal contemporaneity' as the measure of health." [1] And his rejoining of the present and of actuality is demonstrated also by his returning to the United States to do his ogling. He has outlived his Blue Period—his grief at his mother's death—his hatred of the country he has had to return to, and his idealization of his natural feelings toward women.

In so doing, he is renouncing the poseur as he is outliving grief. He who had been in love with his dead mother is acknowledging woman alive (not dead or cloistered). Now that the Blue Period is over, he and we can see it as a passing phase. With him, as with his beloved Picasso (whose well-known, public plight thus illuminates the young man's private plight), grief at the death of a loved one at last wears out. Recovering, he proceeds to the Period of life and love and the flesh as it really is—Rose.

A final word about painters and Salinger's hero. Although a part of his commitment to a Picasso period is affectation, as Salinger appears to want us to understand, what we do not know and are not likely to grasp without effort is De Daumier-Smith's attachment to yet another painter. For if any casual student of art is familiar with the facts of Picasso's Blue Period—of its cause and the form it took in art—it is by no means true that another identification of Smith's at this same time is recognizable except by those who know the history of Italian painting. For De Daumier-Smith tells us that in his letter to Sister Irma "I asked her (and I knew what a long shot it was) if she had ever seen any reproductions of paintings by Antonello da Messina." This is after he has been enraptured by her painting of Christ's burial, a water color whose only serious flaw was the colors used on the faces of the people represented; and it is before the first of his references to Mary Magdalene's being dressed in blue and his remark that "you are too passionate to paint just in water-colours and never in oils indefinitely."

What gives this more than passing interest is the way it parallels what we know of Antonello's life and work. No one who treats Italian painting before the Renaissance omits this fifteenth-century Sicilian, even if only to link him with Bellini. But it is the reasons for his importance that are pertinent here. Foremost is Vasari's crediting him with introducing the art of oil painting into Italy (from the Flemish painters). Equally significant is the tribute of L. Venturi (in his *Origins of Venetian Painting*, 1907): "The white and rose of his flesh colors always have a special coolness . . . consistent and strong, and in this representation of the flesh we find perhaps the clearest expression of Antonello's classicism." Finally, as the color reproductions of Antonello's work that De Daumier-Smith is recommending indicate, Antonello achieves some of his finest effects with blue. Familiar are his *Mary and Child*, with Mary in a blue cape; his large Crucifixion scene, with Mary at the foot of the cross, a blue cape around her on the ground; his *Portrait of a Young Man* with the entire background in blue; and his *St. Jerome in His Study*, in which Jerome is entirely surrounded by blue: blue-figured tiles beneath and on either side of him, blue sky in the windows above. No wonder, then, that these facts, which correspond so closely to those of Sister Irma's work, evoke in her instructor advice so knowledgeably garnered from Antonello's own work.

Salinger's story, whose first part should be read in the light of the facts of Pablo Picasso's life story and professional development, and whose climax is a scene that can be recognized only in connection with a poem of Rainer Maria Rilke's, may be found to contain yet other echoes less sustained but none the less striking and curious, their use again challenging us to define the effects of Salinger's storytelling technique.

First, to return to the scene of initiation in front of the shopwindow. It is possible that, along with its burlesque of Rilke's poem, there is an echo of a scene in the Bible—namely, the one of the conversion of Saul into St. Paul on the road to Damascus. The story is one that Paul tells three times in Acts. On the road (he was going on a wicked mission), suddenly he saw "a light from heaven, above the brightness of the sun." "I could not see for the glory of that light," he recalls, and he fell to the ground. When he arose and "his eyes were opened, he saw no man." With this, compare De Daumier-Smith's experience at night. While he is watching the young woman lace up the truss on the dummy in the window, "I had my Experience. Suddenly . . . the sun came up and sped towards the bridge of my nose at the rate of ninety-three million miles a second. Blinded and very frightened— I had to put my hand on the glass to keep my balance. The thing lasted for no more than a few seconds. When I got my sight back, the girl had gone. . . . I backed away from the window and walked around the block twice, till my knees stopped buckling."

Of the two other possible echoes or allusions, if we consider the first of them—one brief enough to be called fugitive—it is only because the young man himself asks us (or Sister Irma) to. It concerns an incident that occurred in Paris when he was seventeen, on the happiest day of his life. His mother, who had been ill for a long time, had recovered sufficiently to go out, and he was on his way to meet her and have lunch with her, "when suddenly . . . I bumped into a chap without any nose. I ask you to please consider that factor, in fact I beg you. It is quite pregnant with meaning."

Why? The context is a discussion of the necessary connection between the artist's point of view and a slight but constant feeling of unhappiness. We also know that at least one year, at most two, after the day when Salinger's hero's "ecstatically happy" feeling was interrupted by meeting the man with the grotesque face, his mother, who was at the time recovering, did actually die. Since this is so, and since the meeting with the man between her recovery and her death was as important as he says it was, then surely the appearance of the noseless man was an omen of ill. The artist, then, De Daumier-Smith is saying, is always unhappy because his sensitivity finds meanings in apparently meaningless happenings. And this not tragically high price is what she, Sister Irma, will have to resign herself to paying for the privilege of being a true artist.

Now it requires no great insight for us to associate, as the seventeen-year-old De Daumier-Smith seems to have, the face of the noseless man with a death's-head. But if instead of teasing us to find out, as Salinger is doing, just why this meeting on a Paris street was "pregnant with meaning," we had actually associated his noseless face with the famous one of Thomas Mann's in *Death in Venice*, our labors would have been lighter. The man who appears seemingly out of nowhere in Mann's story is standing in the portico of a mortuary chapel. He is exotically dressed and "strikingly snub-nosed" (later, Mann refers to "his little turned-up nose"). Aschenbach—a famous art historian, remember—finds this most pregnant with meaning, as well he might: "True, what he felt was no more than a longing to travel; yet coming upon him with such suddenness and passion as to resemble a seizure, almost a hallucination." His longing to travel is, he senses—just as De Daumier-Smith had sensed—one connected with death, for it leads to a vision of tropical scenes among whose bamboo thicket "the eyes of a crouching tiger gleamed—and he felt his heart throb with terror. . . . Then the vision vanished." We know, by the close of Mann's story, that the vision was prophetic, for it led to Aschenbach's death; we know, if we fit together the pieces of Salinger's story—widely separated though he has them in the story—that his young man's was too, for it led to his mother's death.

Picasso, St. Paul, Rilke, Mann. Finally, and very possibly, Shakespeare as well. His Hamlet finds the noseless face of Yorick pregnant with meaning, and bids Horatio so to inform milady, as De Daumier-Smith does his pupil, Sister Irma. But this parallel with Hamlet—if indeed it is this, too—is merely one, and the weakest at that, of a series of parallels between Shakespeare's play and Salinger's story. Hamlet's father has been dead only three months; so has De Daumier-Smith's mother. The seeming carnality of a widowed parent under such circumstances revolts both Hamlet and De Daumier-Smith. Hamlet puts on an antic disposition; Salinger's character assumes a new identity. Hamlet is, we think, around nineteen years of age and we know that the removal from Wittenberg to provincial Elsinore is distasteful to him; De Daumier-Smith is around nineteen years of age and emphasizes the distastefulness to him of having to leave Paris for New York City. Finally, Ophelia's father, sensing danger to her chastity in Hamlet's mad antics, orders her to break off relations with him; and Sister Irma's "father" cancels her enrollment in Smith's course after the latter's sane-insane letter to her.

One leaves Salinger's story pondering the over-all playfulness, the profusion of literary and biographical allusion and echo detailed above, and is not certain either of the intent or the effect. The self-mockery in this playfulness may be, as was suggested above, the defense of the sensitive against the imputation (even by himself) of sentiment: certainly the story is, without this elaborate overlay, a sentimental one after all. As, looking back at it after the passage of a number of years, the amused and sophisticated autobiographer is at last in a position to admit. The madman can offer only mad utterances and for the analyst only. The once-mad but now sane, however, can give an account of his earlier condition either by analysis or, if he is an artist, by the implicit judgment of echo and allusion put to the uses of comedy. What folly, back then! As though my grief was worthy of comparison with that of the great Picasso! As though what broke my silly spell was deserving of nothing less than Rilke's own reprimand!

And yet it was.

8

The Paving Stones of Paris
Association from Poe
to the Present

As we read indoors in the latter part of the afternoon, the light wanes so gradually that we are not aware; we squint a little and perhaps would go on and on did not someone come in from another room to reveal to us that we are reading in almost utter darkness. This may suggest the situation experienced by the reader as he proceeds from early to late American fiction: during the course of the past century the image of the human mind that he finds there gradually changes from a broad and lucid plane surface to a spherical one bewilderingly marked with inclines, declivities, and fissures; from a precise, logical machine to an imprecise, illogical, and frequently impenetrable thicket of sensations, fears, and obsessions.[1] Particularly is this evident in our conception of the reason for and the way in which our thoughts occur. The paths and bypaths of this changing image from Aristotle to our own day have been charted by William James and later scholars (Melvin Friedman's *Stream of Consciousness*, in particular). The present study limits itself to merely a sketch of the developments of theory about association: its proper province is their application to American literature. By association I mean that important aspect of the thought process termed, since James's day, stream of consciousness: namely, "the symbolizations, the feelings, and the process of association" as Robert Humphrey identifies it.[2]

We may begin our sketch of American literary association where American fiction itself began, with Edgar Allan Poe, who in the course of offering the first fictional demonstration of crime detection made the first measurement and association of ideas in the human mind. The order of these two pioneering steps was actually the reverse, we recall, in "The Murders in the Rue Morgue" (1841). There Poe, in attempting to give plausibility to the ease with which Dupin would shortly pierce the impenetrable veil of the Paris murders, shrewdly prefaced that feat with another. "He is a very little fellow, that's true," Dupin remarks to the nameless predecessor of Dr. Watson, breaking a silence of at least a quarter of an hour and chiming in with X's thoughts, "and would do better for the *Théâtre des Variétés*." When X demands an explanation of this mental wizardry, he is treated to this first chain of association in our literature:

(1) fruiterer
(2) street stones
(3) stereotomy
(4) Epicurus
(5) Dr. Nichols
(6) Orion
(7) Chantilly

Dupin connects these "larger links" for the reader: a fruiterer's thrust having cast X upon a pile of paving stones, his glance was still directed downward when he and Dupin entered a street paved experimentally by the stereotomy method; the second half of this odd term led to the thought of atomies; this, to the nebular theory of Epicurus; this, to the name of its modern corroborator; this, to the great nebula in Orion; finally the change in name from the older spelling, Urion, suggested Chantilly, a cobbler who on assuming the buskin had changed his own name, and about whose shortness X was thinking when Dupin interrupted his thoughts.

Fabulous clairvoyance? Not entirely. For Dupin goes on to point out that he has relied step by step on certain of X's sounds or gestures. Did not X actually mutter the word "stereotomy," look up at the sky to find the great nebula, and finally change his posture from a stoop to one of erectness in thinking of the little cobbler? Moreover, Poe, who was merely setting the stage for his more important feat of logic, apparently had no intention of setting himself up as an expert on the processes of human thought. But since, hocus-pocus or not, Dupin's explanation must be thought of as reflecting (if not formulating) the thinking of its day, it may be examined as a rare example of association in its infancy.

What concerns us here are the association principles which Poe was implicitly positing. These will be seen to be: (1) the exceeding slowness of the process of ideas in association; (2) the supremacy, if not the entirety, of recency in association of ideas: as X pointedly remarks earlier, he has literally neither seen nor conversed with anyone except Dupin for several months; and every link in the chain of X's thoughts can be seen to have been forged during this brief period; (3) the nonexistence of capricious associative bypaths; the absence of recurring themes.

The first of these would seem to merit little comment here, for it is unsuited to fiction per se. The most patently dated of Poe's suppositions, it was the first to be displaced.[3] Forty years later, Sir Francis Galton was to perform on himself an experiment in terms of voluntary association of ideas which revealed that "It took a total time of 660 seconds to form . . . 505 ideas; that is, at about the rate of 50 in one minute or 3000 in an hour." This, he pointed out in his book, "would be miserably slow work in reverie, or wherever the thought follows in the lead of each association that successively presents itself." Such a scientific report would be expected to completely discredit Dupin's claim that X's mind had forged only seven links in a revery lasting fifteen minutes.

Moreover, Galton's accompanying report would surely be counted upon to discourage any further amateurish feats of mind reading *pari passu*. His associated ideas, he insisted, were mostly due to his own unshared experiences, and consequently could neither coincide with those of a second person repeating the experiment nor enable the latter to record them. The cleavage beginning, as it must, with the first thought, not parallel lines would result but widely diverging ones.[4] "If we take as the associative starting-point . . . some simple word which I pronounce before you," William James told Cambridge teachers in 1892, "there is no limit to the possible diversity of suggestions which it may set up in your minds." Even more bafflingly, "In the same person, the same word heard at different times will provoke, in consequence of the varying marginal preoccupations, [any] one of a number of diverse possible associative sequences." That, he concluded, is why "we can never cipher out in advance just what the person will be thinking of five minutes later."[5]

Yet half a century after Poe, Conan Doyle, surely unaware of the repudiation to his admitted literary progenitor implicit in Galton's findings, imitated Dupin's trick (which he held lightly) in "The Resident Patient." Here Holmes confounds Watson by remarking, entirely apropos, after a silence, "You're right,

Watson. . . . It does seem a preposterous way of settling a dispute." He has parsed Watson's revery as follows:

(1) General Gordon
(2) Henry Ward Beecher
(3) Beecher's mission to England in wartime
(4) American Civil War
(5) Anglo-Afghanistan fighting
(6) international entanglements.

Like Dupin, Holmes is prouder of his detection of the clues provided by his unwitting subject than by his own mind reading. Watson's eyes revealed his attention to the newly framed picture of General Gordon, then to the unframed portrait of Beecher; his glance at the wall indicated to Holmes his reflection that if framed the Beecher would just cover a bare space and correspond with the Gordon; in gazing at Beecher, Watson's look was hard, his eyes puckered, and his face was thoughtful, indicating successive thoughts about Beecher's career, his mission to England, and his uncivil reception there; the sparkle in Watson's eyes meant thoughts about the American Civil War; the set of his lips, the look in his eyes, and the clenching of his hands, thoughts of American gallantry; his sadness and headshaking, thoughts about the sadness, horror, and useless waste of life in war; his hand stealing to his own old wound, reminiscence of his fighting in Afghanistan; and finally the smile quivering on his lips, thoughts about the ridiculous side of this method of settling international questions.

Although they are similar, it will be evident later that Conan Doyle's association, so far from advancing Poe's, is far less realistic, and by comparison makes the older feat seem modern, which it is not. There is, to be sure, one reference to Watson's own private (i.e., pre-Holmesian) past, and this is worth noting; but Holmes was quite familiar with Watson's military career, and in every other respect the links are very much like X's: ideas common to all thinking men or familiar to Holmes on the necessarily special terms of his close association with Watson.

This more or less describes the association of ideas Mark Twain attributes to the river-pilot Brown in *Life on the Mississippi*. Twain elaborates it for the purpose of illustrating the omnivorous indiscrimination of the man's memory (like that of the informant in the "Celebrated Jumping Frog" story) as he started to tell a funny story about a dog:

> . . . his memory would start with the dog's breed and personal appearance; drift into a history of his owner; of his owner's family, with descriptions of weddings and burials that had occurred in it, together with recitals of congratulatory verses and obituary poetry provoked by the same; then this memory would recollect that one of these events occurred during the celebrated "hard winter" of such-and-such a year, and a minute description of that winter would follow, along with the names of people who were frozen to death, and statistics showing the high figures which pork and hay went up to. Pork and hay would suggest corn and fodder; corn and fodder would suggest cows and horses; cows and horses would suggest the circus and certain celebrated bareback riders; the transition from the circus to the menagerie was easy and natural; from the elephant to equatorial Africa was but a step; then of course the heathen savages would suggest religion; and at the end of three or four hours' tedious jaw, . . . Brown would [be] muttering extracts from sermons he had heard years before about the efficacy of prayer as a means of grace.[6]

When in 1888 the first stream-of-consciousness novel was appearing serially, George Moore, while encouraging its author, Édouard Dujardin, worried to him that the new technique might result in monotony.[7] In the above passage, Moore's fear is already confirmed, though presenting the monotony of the consciousness of a bore was precisely Twain's purpose in allowing us to follow Brown's thoughts as they poured out.

The point relevant to this discussion is, of course, not the imputed clairvoyance of Dupin or Holmes or the garrulity of Twain's bore, but the exact description of the chains of thought which they were reproducing: the contemporary assumptions about association which their creators were fabricating or to which they were tacitly subscribing. In any event, if Conan Doyle appears to be the last writer of fiction to have enabled one character to lay another's mind bare in the association process, it is no wonder; for psychology, and then psychoanalysis, would soon take over association from fiction and philosophy, and record its findings in such more likely places as reports of experiments and case histories (which fiction, in turn, would make use of).

And in truth any attempt to evaluate Poe's two other, more important, premises leads us back to where fiction would have had to go and to where psychology did go to find the roots of association theory—to philosophy. For all such theorizing seems to derive from Aristotle and come down through Hobbes, Hume, and Hartley to William James, its famous expositor and historian,[8] and to Sigmund Freud, who in turn took it from the laboratory into the clinic.

Actually, it was Poe's own predecessor and master Coleridge who, in correcting Hartley, both traced the principles of association back to Aristotle and first suggested the direction which it would take in the future. Aristotle's general law of association, Cole-

ridge points out, is this: "Ideas, by having been together, acquire a power of recalling each other; or every
partial representation awakes the total representation
of which it had been a part." In applying this general
principle to individual recollections, Aristotle admitted "five agents or occasioning causes: 1st, connection
in time, whether simultaneous, preceding or successive; 2d, vicinity or connection in space; 3d, interde-
pendence or necessary connection, as cause and effect;
4th, likeness; and 5th, contrast." The principle of
contemporaneity, "which Aristotle had made the
common condition of all the laws of association, Hartley was constrained to represent as being itself the
sole law," Coleridge writes. Now if this is true, he
continues, it is true only of a state of "absolute delirium" or of "complete light headedness." Take, for
example, a total impression of St. Paul's. Only to a
madman might every partial representation of the
scene "recall the total of the infinite number of com-
ponent parts of the total representation." Similarly,
the illiterate girl who accurately reproduced aloud ancient and learned texts impressed on her mind some
years before while in the employ of a scholar did so
and could do so only in a state of delirium. Such feats
are impossible to the normal man because they are
performable only in the absence of "all interference of
the will, reason, and judgment." In thus substantiating
Aristotle, Coleridge provides a paradigm of his own:

(1) mackerel
(2) gooseberries
(3) goose
(4) swan.

The sight of the mackerel might suggest gooseberries,
which formed the sauce eaten with the fish; and the
first syllable of the word gooseberries might suggest

the fowl itself; and this, a swan (albeit he had never seen the two species together). "In the two former instances, I am conscious that their co-existence in time was the circumstance that enabled me to recollect them; and equally conscious am I, that the latter was recalled to me by the joint operation of likeness and contrast. So it is with cause and effect; so too with order." [9]

Even though it exposes Hartley's fallacy, Coleridge's brief chain of association, it can be seen, consists of links even simpler than Poe's. And in truth Coleridge no more than Poe conceived a chain wherein the true and private bypaths of normal human thought would be made manifest. This would await the revelations of psychologists late in the century. Coleridge does loom large in the history of association theory, however, for a different reason. Not only does his servant girl anticipate the Freud-Breuer initial recorded case analysis of hysteria, but his insistence on a kind of censor—"the will, reason, and judgment"—as a dividing line between completely uninhibited and "normal" association gave prominence to a conception which we usually attribute to our own times. As Coleridge summed up his own "true practical general law of association": "[Whatever] makes certain parts of a total impression more vivid or distinct than the rest, will determine the mind to recall these, in preference to others equally linked together by the common condition of contemporaneity, or . . . continuity. But the will itself, by confining and intensifying the attention, may arbitrarily give vividness to any object whatsoever." [10] Now it is this voluntary interruption of the association of ideas that will appear later in the century in an inverse but still recognizable form.

Meanwhile it takes us a long way toward that important spokesman and "father" of psychology, William James. And James's theories, it appears, look in both directions. In one important respect he seems to fall into step with such suppositions of association as were found in Poe and Conan Doyle. Here is a revery of his and his paradigm of it:

(1) clock
(2) clock repairman
(3) jeweler's shop (where James last saw him)
(4) (gold) shirt studs (bought at the shop)
(5) value of gold, and its decline
(6) equal value of greenbacks
(7) Bayard resolution in Senate about legal-tender notes.

This example of what he calls Ordinary, or Mixed, association resembles those of Poe and Coleridge.[11] But note his analysis: for to the significant question "Why did the jeweller's shop suggest the shirt-studs rather than a chain . . . bought there more recently, which had cost more, and whose sentimental associations were more interesting?" he answers, "Accident." It must have been that "the stud-tract happened at that moment to lie more open, either because of some accidental alteration in its nutrition or because the incipient subconscious tensions of the brain as a whole had so distributed their equilibrium that it was more unstable here than in the chain-tract." Thus he is led to conclude that "to a certain extent, even in those forms of ordinary mixed association which lie nearest to impartial redintegration, *which* associate of the interesting item shall emerge must be called largely a matter of accident—accident, that is, for our intelligence." Here is the step which James took beyond Coleridge's, for in place of Coleridge's "will, reason, and judgment" has been substituted a hypothetical neurological tension, and more than that—un-reason itself. At "transitions of reason," in fact, James scoffs. Reason, he insists, "is only one out of a thousand possibilities in the thinking of each of us." Then, in a purely rhetorical question, he uttered this challenge: "Who can count all the silly fancies, the grotesque suppositions, the utterly irrelevant reflections he makes in the course of a day?" [12]

James Joyce would respond to this challenge a generation later, yet one wonders whether Edgar Allan Poe might not have been able to half a century before, had he set himself to it. For it was Poe who had premised a principle of human conduct of which the psychology of his day, he said, "takes no account," which causes man to do not that which reason requires but reason's opposite—the principle of the perverse. Thus the hero of "The Black Cat" refuses to allow the police to depart his premises before he compulsively draws their attention to his crime. And in "The Imp of the Perverse" this "innate and primitive principle of human action" this "paradoxical something" ("Through its promptings we act, for the reason that we should *not*. In theory, no reason can be more unreasonable; but, in fact, there is none more strong.") causes the hero, years after committing a murder, to confess it to the police. Why, we may wonder, does Poe not apply this principle to the thought-by-thought, split-second, functioning of the human mind? Then he would have created a form of fiction superior to the detective story "The Murders in the Rue Morgue"—the form, more exactly, that Molly Bloom's revery at the close of *Ulysses* takes—even if, to be sure, one not nearly so satisfying to the readers of fiction of his day.

Meanwhile, simultaneously with James's, Galton's findings were leading to a similar surrender to the

force of unreason. His experiments on himself, he
confessed, gave him a surprising insight into the "obscure depths" in which the operations of the mind
take place. The general impression they left on him
was like that which many people experience when the
basement of their house first undergoes major repair:
then "we realize for the first time the complex system
of drains and gas and water pipes, flues, bell-wires, and
so forth, upon which our comfort depends, but . . .
with whose experience, so long as they acted well, we
had never troubled ourselves." Exposed for the first
time were old, seemingly discarded data such as "Bib-
lical scraps, family expressions, bits of poetry, and the
like" in great number. These, he said, "rise to the
thoughts so quickly, whenever anything suggests them,
that they commonly outstrip all competitors." [13] And
Oliver Wendell Holmes, who combined the practice
of medicine with the writing of prose, fiction, and
poetry, reflected that "We know very little of the
contents of our minds until some sudden jar brings
them to light, as an earthquake that shakes down a
miser's house brings out the old stockings full of gold,
and all the hoards that have hid away in holes and
crannies." [14] In short, the emphasis in association
theory has increasingly been on the importance of
chance, or unreason; on what Thomas Wolfe, borrowing from Matthew Arnold, would call on the title page
of his first novel, "the buried life."

Before we go forward from this point, we should
pause for a backward look. Whereas it is true that Poe
had given a lecture on association that today we
would consider naïve, it is also true that if we consider
an American fiction contemporaneous with "The
Murders in the Rue Morgue," we will be impressed
with the ability of tellers of tales to anticipate science
and we will be minded of Freud's generous confession

concerning them. Turn to the long paragraph just before the close of Chapter 2 of *The Scarlet Letter*. Here Hawthorne takes us inside the mind of the anguished young woman branded an adulteress and standing on the scaffold in the Boston marketplace serving her punishment of public humiliation. From her place, Hawthorne tells us, she commands a point of view of "the entire track along which she had been treading since her happy infancy." She sees the village in which she had been born in England, the house where she lived, her father's face, her mother's, her own; then the elderly man she had unwisely married, his eyes and his deformed body; then the streets and buildings of Amsterdam, the interim abode of the Prynnes; and "lastly" she sees the rude marketplace of the Puritan settlement where she is now standing in the gaze of the populace: "Yes!—these were her realities—all else had vanished!"

If this were all that our first psychological novelist represented as the thoughts of a woman in Hester's mental state and the order in which they occurred, our estimation of his grasp of association would be no greater than that of Poe's, whose unveiling of X's mind had revealed a similarly limited, ordered, and chronological train of thought. But it happens that the sequence of Hester's thoughts that we have just been treated to is merely a sequel to, an ordering of, a highly disorderly stream of thought that Hawthorne himself has just presented in the paragraph preceding. In this paragraph he reveals a grasp of knowledge of association that we usually ascribe to the psychologists who came after him.[15] For what Hester sees during certain "intervals" is a scene that "glimmered indistinctly" to a mind "preternaturally active" because of the unbearable tension to which it is being subjected. In fact, the "other scenes" and "other faces" that crowd into the present sound very much like the ones Galton has just found in his own present: "Reminiscences the most trifling and immaterial, passages of infancy and school-days, sports, childish quarrels, and the little domestic traits of her maiden years, came swarming back upon her, intermingled with recollections of whatever was gravest in her subsequent life; one picture precisely as vivid as another; as if all were of similar importance, or all alike a play." And, as though this were not in itself most impressive in a novelist of 1850, Hawthorne lingers over it in an attempt to account for the hash it makes of time and place: "Possibly, it was an instinctive device of her spirit, to relieve itself, by the exhibition of these phantasmagoric forms, from the cruel weight and hardness of the reality." [16]

As an interpretation of his heroine's mental activity in terms of repression and sublimation before there were such terms, the above sentence is most impressive. In fact, as regards its scientific bent, almost as impressive as the demonstration of his hero's thought processes by Sherwood Anderson in *Dark Laughter* (1925) and of his explanation of those processes, doubtless influenced by Freud. Here are the associated thoughts of the hero, as presented in the second chapter:

(1) John Stockton
(2) "Bruce, Smart and Feeble — Hardware"
(3) "Dudley Brothers — Grocery"
(4) Bruce Dudley
(5) Captain Bruce Dudley American Army; Reverend Bruce Dudley, Minister of the First Presbyterian Church, Hartford, Conn.
(6) "T'witchelty, T'weedlety, T'wadelty, T'wum, Catch a nigger by the thumb, eh?"

The transformation of John Stockton into Bruce Dudley takes place at an Illinois town on the Mississippi River. He is en route to Old Harbor, on the Ohio River, where he had lived as a boy. Needing a new name to escape recognition by the older residents of Old Harbor, he appropriates it from elements of two signs he sees on stores in the Illinois town. There are questions prompted by his making the change that he gropes for. Others are left to the reader. But the key to all the associations, he discovers, is Mark Twain.

Why Hartford? Because Mark Twain had lived there a long time, he says. Why a minister? Because there had been a connection between Twain and a Presbyterian (or Congregational or Baptist) minister there, he says. If he knows it, he seems only subconsciously aware of this, that the name of the minister in Hartford was Twitchell, the name that appears slightly altered in the doggerel that comes to his mind. Why think of Mark Twain? Because Stockton realized that for six months he has been traveling, like Twain, on the Mississippi River. Because—as he may or may not realize—Mark Twain was also an adopted name, and also connected with the river. Because so much of Twain's *Huckleberry Finn* concerned Negroes, who had occupied so much of Stockton's thoughts while on the river. And because, in an exact antithesis, whereas Twain had taken on a new and more respectable identity in his life and associations in Hartford, now he, Stockton, is sloughing off his old respectability with his old name and assuming a new and unshackled one in moving to Old Harbor as Bruce Dudley. As he concludes his own analysis of his change of identity: "It wasn't strange after all that he chanced to think of Hartford, Connecticut. . . . 'He did get all crusted up, that boy [Twain],' he whispered to himself that day when he went about the streets of the Illinois town bearing for the first time the name

Bruce Dudley." Going East had ruined Twain. " 'A man like that, eh—who had seen what that man had, a man who could write and feel and think like that *Huckleberry Finn*, going up there to Hartford and —.' " Thus do boyhood reading and present actions flow together and interact with adult, critical reading; thus does much that is remote and mysterious reveal itself completely by the bright light of introspection and analysis: in his own person Anderson would soon confide that Stockton's judgment about Twain's change after he moved to Hartford had been borrowed from Van Wyck Brooks' *The Ordeal of Mark Twain* (1920).[17] In the sophistication of its association, this chapter of Anderson's story unquestionably advances beyond Hawthorne's brief paragraph; yet the difference is one of degree, rather than of kind. And as regards the plausibility of the causation each author ascribes to his character's mental activity, there is little difference at all.

But Hawthorne's accomplishment was a rare one for his times: it is to the present century, to Sherwood Anderson's contemporaries that we must look for the incorporation into fiction of such findings as Galton's and James's. Their influence can be seen at work in the fiction of James Joyce, to cite the most influential of all. How far we have come from Poe's (or even James's) comparatively lucid, circumscribed mental meanderings can be demonstrated on many pages of *Ulysses*. Consider the revery of Leopold Bloom as he returns from his morning shopping in the second chapter (the work of how few seconds or split seconds of association we can guess from the composition of Joyce's prose).

> The sun was nearing the steeple of George's church. Be a warm day I fancy. Specially in these black clothes feel it more. Black conducts, reflects (refracts is it?), the heat. But I couldn't go in that light suit. Make a picnic

of it. . . . Boland's breadvan delivering with trays our daily but she prefers yesterday's loaves turnovers crisp crowns hot. Makes you feel young. Somewhere in the east: early morning: set off at dawn, travel round in front of the sun, steal a day's march on him. Keep it up for ever, never grow a day older technically. Walk along a strand, strange land, come to a city gate, sentry there, old ranker too, old Tweedy's big moustaches leaning on a long kind of spear.

Brief as this cut-off length of Bloom's interior monologue is, in it the reader can perceive the rapier-like flicks of the mind, the interweavings in time and space, the pell-mell rush of ideas piling up on each other even in what is indicated as one sentence. The warm sun of the present moment spins into the timelessness of a law of physics into a self-defense of his wearing black in preparation for a funeral that afternoon (the future); the vision of a bread truck in the present metamorphoses into a part of a prayer from boyhood, shifting suddenly to his wife's taste in bread —all in one sentence; back to the sun's warmth, into a hypothetical and fantastic application of Einsteinian physics about light and time; next into phraseology from poetry or romance, into a vision of far, exotic lands, into that of his father-in-law, now dead, who had served in the Mediterranean.

Joyce's book, a declaration of independence from all taboos, ranging from the rhetorical (sentence structure and punctuation) to the biological (genito-urinary), was immensely influential in ambitious American fiction, notably in the first novel of Thomas Wolfe. Here, as a random example, is the monologue of Oliver Gant as he muses on his return to Altamont from a trip to California:

America's Switzerland. The beautiful Land of the Sky. Jesus God! Old Bowman said he'll be a rich man some day. Built up all the way to Pasadena. Come on out. Too late now. Think he was in love with her. No matter. Too old. Wants her out there. No fool like— white bellies of the fish. A spring somewhere to wash me through. Clean as a baby once more. New Orleans, the night Jim Corbett knocked out John L. Sullivan. The man who tried to rob me. My clothes and my watch. Five blocks down Canal Street in my night-gown. Two A.M. Threw them all in a heap—watch landed on top. Fight in my room. Town full of crooks and pick-pockets for prize-fight. Make good story. Policeman half hour later. They come out and beg you to come in. Frenchwomen. Creoles. Beautiful Creole heiress. Steamboat race. Captain, they are gaining. I will not be beaten. Out of wood. Use the bacon she said proudly. There was a terrific explosion. He got her as she sank the third time and swam to shore. They powder in front of the window, smacking their lips at you. For old men better maybe. Who gets the business there? Bury them all above ground. Water two feet down. Rots them. Why not? All big jobs. Italy. Carrara and Rome. Yet Brutus is an honorable man. What's a Creole? French and Spanish. Has she any nigger blood? Ask Cardiac? [18]

A gloss of this apparently momentary snake's coil of reflections would disclose mental interweavings in time and space, reality and phantasy very much like those of Joyce's. Local publicity slogans; an allusion to the name of the avenue up which Gant is traveling; a former friend visited in California; the latter's enthusiasm for his new home; Gant's regrets; Bowman's affair; half of a familiar adage; the whiteness of fish in California waters; water; water as purifier and rejuvenator; an incident of fourteen years before in New Orleans when robbers had left him almost as naked as a baby; New Orleans prostitutes; phantasy about Creoles probably interwoven with a plot from shoddy fiction; prostitutes again; their antics; sexual practices and old men; death; death in a city where water is close beneath the earth; big grave contracts (Gant is a stonecutter); Italy as home of grave stone; Mark Antony's phrase; definition of a Creole; deliberation about an Altamont dark-skin (associated with Bowman above?); and finally back to an Altamont doctor.

While allowing for the fact that Wolfe's massive detail merely puts into practice the theory advanced by Hawthorne in his general statement about Hester Prynne's train of thought, and that the center of consciousness of a worldly middle-aged man of the twentieth century can be expected to yield much forbidden to that of the virgin of the nineteenth, still we can measure the progress that had been made toward complete exposition of the depths of human thought in the process of association by comparing the uninhibited Gant with Phoebe Pyncheon's (which is to say, Hawthorne's) refusal to intrude upon certain of Clifford Pyncheon's thoughts (and these, the thoughts of a worldly man) in *The House of the Seven Gables*: "When he is cheerful—when the sun shines into his mind—then I venture to peep in, just as far as the light reaches, but no further. It is holy ground where the shadow falls." [19]

All these, of course, are waking trains of thought. Now the nineteenth-century French psychologist Ribot, in insisting that "this law of association is the truly fundamental, irreducible phenomenon of our mental life," that "it is at the bottom of all our acts," that "it permits of no exception," and that no human experience can be without it, does not except such experience as "dream, revery, mystic ecstasy, nor the most abstract reasoning." [20] And one of the foundation stones of Freud's psychoanalysis, even more important clinically than the free association of the patient awake, is the value of contents of dreams in revealing this unconscious thought. Indeed, *The Interpretation of Dreams*, appearing in eight different versions over a period of thirty years, may have been responsible for the prominence of Freud's name more than any other of his publications. At the start, he submitted that to understand morbid states of mind, one must explain the origin of dream-images. This, in 1900. But from the beginning, writers had found dreams a fascinating and irresistible area of mental activity, yielding, to the proper touch, who knew what secrets about the human psyche. Many centuries before, Lucretius and Seneca had speculated about dreams, as Freud himself reminds us.[21] Ralph Waldo Emerson had proposed in "Nature" (1836) that the mysteries of his age, dreams among them, were merely unexplained, not unexplainable. His neighbor, Nathaniel Hawthorne, anticipating Freud, had commented in "The Birthmark" (1843) that "The mind is in a sad state when Sleep, the all-involving, cannot confine her spectres within the dim region of her sway, but suffers them to break forth, affrighting this actual life with secrets that perchance belong to a deeper one." Not even in sleep could Aylmer keep from betraying to his young wife his secret and obsessive desire to remove the tiny hand from her cheek. "Truth often finds its way to the mind close muffled in robes of sleep, and then speaks with uncompromising directness of matters in regard to which we practise an unconscious self-deception during our waking moments." General and allusive though these observations of Hawthorne's may be, they strike one today as in advance of their time, as heralding the findings of the next century, when the practitioner of the New Psychology would feel obliged to "turn to the unconscious, which we have with us so conspicuously eight hours out of every twenty-four that even the most benighted recognise it, and which is inconspicuously with us always." As Frederick J. Hoffman would later point out, the dream is the area of expression "that has so impressed and interested the poet and novelist, has opened up new possibilities for the expression of unconscious states in fiction." [22]

In Hawthorne's own time, to be sure, Flaubert can be seen making a brief approach to this new area of experience. Here, in a passage reminiscent of Hawthorne's account of Hester's thoughts on the scaffold at the beginning of *The Scarlet Letter*, is Charles Bovary setting out sleepily around 4:00 A.M. to the farm of the Bertaux to set Monsieur Rouault's broken leg: "Charles from time to time opened his eyes, his mind grew weary, and sleep coming upon him, he soon fell into a doze wherein his recent sensations blending with memories, he became conscious of a double self, at once student and married man, lying in his bed as but now, and crossing the operation theatre as of old. The warm smell of poultices mingled in his brain with the fresh odour of dew; he heard the iron rings rattling along the curtain-rods of the bed and saw his wife sleeping." But what we are looking at here is what Leon Edel finds in Balzac, namely the writer "contenting himself with a mere digest from the moment he seeks to deal with subjective material. . . . The novelists of the nineteenth century . . . agreed that subjective states could be *reported* but not *rendered* in the novel." [23] Hawthorne had wistfully admitted this ("Up to this old age of the world, no such thing [as a dream] has ever been written"); yet curiously he had at least pointed the way for the next century, and in his *American Notebooks* had even suggested to its writers the difficulty of steering a course between reality and art: "To write a dream which shall resemble the real course of a dream, with all its inconsistency, its strange transformations, which are all taken as a matter of course, its eccentricities and aimlessness—with nevertheless a leading idea running through the whole." Again, it remained for the present century to take its cue from science and art and, suiting style to subject matter, to attempt to render the material of dreams directly, in the form of thoughts as they actually occur to the dreamer, rather than merely as they are described by the author. This is what Hemingway attempted in the dream sequence of Chapter 28 of *A Farewell to Arms* (1929). Again, it is between midnight and morning, and the physical condition of the character is similar to Flaubert's:

> Both the girls seemed cheered.
> I left them sitting together with Aymo sitting back in the corner and went back to Piani's car. The column of vehicles did not move but the troops kept passing alongside. It was still raining hard and I thought some of the stops in the movement of the column might be from cars with wet wiring. More likely they were from horses or men going to sleep. Still, traffic could tie up in cities when every one was awake. It was the combination of horse and motor vehicles. They did not help each other any. The peasants' carts did not help much either. Those were a couple of fine girls with Barto. A retreat was no place for two virgins. Real virgins. Probably very religious. If there were no war we would probably all be in bed. In bed I lay me down my head. Bed and board. Stiff as a board in bed. Catherine was in bed now between two sheets, over her and under her. Which side did she sleep on? Maybe she wasn't asleep. Maybe she was lying thinking about me. Blow, blow, ye western wind. Well, it blew and it wasn't the small rain but the big rain down that rained. It rained all night. You knew it rained down that rained. Look at it. Christ, that my love were in my arms and I in my bed

again. That my love Catherine. That my sweet love Catherine down might rain. Blow her again to me. Well, we were in it. Every one was caught in it and the small rain would not quiet it. "Good-night, Catherine," I said out loud.

Catherine silently converses with him, then Piani wakes him up by exclaiming an obscenity, ending Frederick's "dream in English" and fairly ambitious venture into association.

The girls referred to at the start of the above passage have sought refuge in Aymo's car and are rebuffing Aymo's insistent advances. (This, before he desists, in deference to their announced virginity.) Frederick Henry, through whose eyes we see the story, is weary. It has been raining for days. He is sick with longing for Catherine, now pregnant with his child. These are the ingredients for the indistinctly coherent dream sequence that now emerges. It seems to begin midway in the passage, probably at the words "Real virgins," where the normal-length sentences, giving way to short ones, have now become mere fragments. Its substance is predictably a mixture of past and present, of near and far, of conscious and unconscious awareness. Against the background of the continuous and depressing rain, his mind produces an image from boyhood, the prayer fragment "In bed I lay me down my head." "Bed" leads to its part in the traditional components of the marriage contract, "bed and board," which introduces the sexual theme responsible for the beginning of the sequence and its continuation to its conclusion.[24] "Bed" having produced "board," "board" now produces the familiar male complaint about female frigidity, "Stiff as a board in bed," that echoes Frederick's earlier, waking observations about the older of the two girls in Aymo's car ("I felt her stiffen when I touched her. . . . Every-

time [Aymo] said the [obscene] word the girl stiffened
a little. Then sitting stiffly . . ."); and this apparently, by contrast, to thoughts of Catherine (who is
anything but unresponsive to him in bed); then to the
familiar anonymous lyric:

> *Western wind, when wilt thou blow?*
> *The small rain down doth rain—*
> *Christ, if my love were in my arms*
> *And I in my bed again!*

Now the timeless (lyric) and the timely (Catherine)
merge, in syntax as well as in thought. From association with Tennyson's song from *The Princess*
("Wind of the western sea! . . . Blow him again to
me") results "Blow her again to me." A reflection on
the universality of the evil that is war (*it*) yields to a
spoken good-night to Catherine; then Frederick's
dream conversation with her is ended by Piani.

In Hemingway's dream passage I think that we can
recognize a degree of what Edmund Wilson calls "the
special kind of language which people speak in
dreams," consisting of garbled elements that "betray
by their telescopings of words, their combinations of
incongruous ideas, the involuntary preoccupations of
the sleeper," which Freud and his followers explored.
Wilson supposes that from them James Joyce appro-
priated the idea for literary use, and that the effects
achieved by this new method as employed in *Finne-
gans Wake* are those which the poetry of symbolism
strives for and that the psychological principles they
employ "give them a new basis in humanity." *Finne-
gans Wake* is almost entirely written in it.[25]

The thoughts of the mind awake, of the mind in
sleep, and eventually even of the abnormal mentality.

William Faulkner's *The Sound and the Fury*, "one of the few really important experimental works of fiction done in America," Oscar Cargill believes, is told through four points of view, the story creating its most ambitious effect in the first, that of a thirty-three-year-old idiot. "Benjy, the idiot and . . . Luster, are hunting golf balls along what was once the Compson pasture fence when a remark addressed by a golfer to his caddie sets off a train of thought in the mind of the idiot, related first to Caddy, his sister, and then to scattered episodes in thirty years of Compson family history. Extraordinary ingenuity is exercised so that these episodes should recur in the mind of Benjy by no more than what would appear to be the most casual association." [26] Literally the first part of Faulkner's story fulfills the promise of the original source of its title. From this it is only a short step up to the last development possible to American fiction, to the story told by a madman. But if this is also a step back to the first development, to Edgar Allan Poe's narrators, now there is an added dimension.

> They're out there.
> Black boys in white suits up before me to commit sex acts in the hall and get it mopped up before I can catch them. . . .
> Stick a mop in my hand and motion to the spot they aim for me to clean today, and I go. . . .
> "Haw, you look at 'im shag it? Big enough to eat apples off my head an' he mine me like a baby."

These are the opening lines of Ken Kesey's *One Flew Over the Cuckoo's Nest* (1962). The narrator is a six-foot-seven-inch tall half-Indian from Oregon named Bromden, a long-time psychotic patient familiar with electro-therapy and related horrors, whose mind flashes in and out of lucidity, of the nightmares of the present and the pleasures of the sanity of the past.

The buried ideas. More than this, the buried senses as well. For the first time, "novelists were seeking to find words that would convey elusive and evanescent thought: not only the words that come to the mind, but the images of the inner world of fantasy, fusing with sounds and smells, the world of perceptual experience." [27] "Odors have an altogether peculiar force, in affecting us through association," Poe had noted briefly long before.[28] And now George Moore would confide to his readers the mysteriously far-reaching effects the sounds of certain names had on his development. He found a "magic" in the sound of Shelley ("that crystal name") that, unaccountably, he could not find in Byron, whose poetry he also was fond of reading. As for the word France, it "rang in my ears and gleamed in my eyes." Years later, when another, a third, magic word sounded, he recalled the effect of the first two: "Echo-augury! Words heard in an unexpected quarter, but applying marvellously well to the besetting difficulty of the moment." The reader will remember "the instant effect the word 'Shelley' had upon me in childhood, and how it called into existence a train of feeling that illuminated the vicissitudes and passions of many years, until it was finally assimilated and became part of my being"; and he will also remember "how the mere mention, at a certain moment, of the word 'France' awoke a vital impulse, even a sense of final ordination, and how the irrevocable message was obeyed, and how it led to the creation of a mental existence." [29]

Odors, sounds, even tastes. Thus Henry Adams in his *Education* recalling his first school years: ". . . the children knew the taste of everything they saw or touched from pennyroyal . . . to . . . the letters of a spelling book—the taste of A-B, AB, suddenly revived on [my] tongue sixty years afterwards." And most prominently of all modern writers, Marcel Proust, by way of finding a self-justification for dedicating his last years to his novel, in its closing pages raised such buried sense associations to the level of ecstasy: the taste of a cake dipped in tea recalling the whole world of his boyhood years at Combray; the sound of a spoon carelessly banged against a plate recalling a forest scene only a few hours before; the touch of a napkin recalling the towel he had used before in drying himself on his first day in Balbec; and the uneven adjoining paving stones of Paris suggesting, not, as to Poe's Mr. X, merely the idea of a local and contemporaneous invention but the physical sensation of a moment years before in the baptistry in St. Mark's in Venice. In following such chains of association as these, something more uncanny than Poe's master-logician Dupin or Conan Doyle's Holmes would be needed. Something, for that matter, more effective than any Geiger counter or radar screen yet devised.

At this point, art would perforce halt, while science went on into the furthest reaches of the human mind. For Coleridge's "will, reason, and judgment"—the barrier between comparatively coherent association and light-headedness or delirium—would emerge refurbished and redocumented in modern psychological theory in such terms as repression and ego and censor. Psychology, now aware that the processes of association, grotesquely free as they are, at times suffer apparently unaccountable blocks, began to perceive that some real force in the subconscious was operating to halt these processes; in short, that the free play of the conscious mind was occasionally thwarted by a hidden obstacle. To William James this phenomenon, a kind of cerebral stuttering, was curious and puzzling, and if his explanation seems extemporized, his example is none the less valuable. He has singled out two verses from "Locksley Hall":

"I, the heir of all *the ages* in the foremost files of time,"
and
"For I doubt not through *the ages* one increasing purpose runs."

Why is it, he asks, that when the person reciting gets as far as "the ages" in the first quotation his mind does not supply the wrong concluding tetrameter? Because the word *following* "the ages" has had its brain process awakened not only by "the ages" but by the brain process of all the words *preceding* "the ages." " '*In*' and not '*one*' or any other word will be the next to awaken, for its brain-process has previously vibrated in unison not only with that of *ages*, but with that of all those other words whose activity is dying away. It is a good case of the effectiveness over thought of what we called . . . a 'fringe.' " So far, James's explanation recalls that of the clock-and-studs paradigm. It is at this point, however, that he goes on to point out the block possible and to account for it in terms that suggest the unsuspected potentialities of the mind in the association process. What might happen, he asks, if the reciter were awaiting the opening of a will which might make him the *heir* of a million? Probably the normal path of discharge would be interrupted at the word "heir." "His *emotional interest in that word* would be such that its *own special associations would prevail* over the combined ones of the other words. He would, as we say, be abruptly reminded of his personal situation, and the poem would lapse altogether from his thoughts." [30]

Freud took the Aristotelian concept restated and illustrated by Coleridge and enlarged by James to include "emotional" subconscious aberrations, and equipped the explanation of such aberrations with a new and respectable word (*repression*) and a new and scandalous factor (sex). Like Galton, Freud turned his examination inward upon his own mental processes and explored what he called, *The Psychopathology of Everyday Life*. What monstrous fish may be swimming about deep below the surface of our apparently proper minds his paradigm of the "psychic mechanism of forgetfulness" clearly illustrates. Trying to recall the name of a certain painter, he could think only of two others, neither of whom was nearly as familiar to him. Finally he identified the block as one occasioned by an incident of sexual disturbance. Whereupon he concluded that the name-forgetting could no longer be considered accidental, that there was a motive interrupting his thoughts and causing him to exclude from his consciousness the thought which might have led his mind to the sexual incident: "that is, I wanted to forget something, I *repressed* something. To be sure, I wished to forget something other than the name; but this other thought brought about an associative connection between itself and this name, so that my act of volition missed the aim, and I *forgot the one against my will*, while I intentionally wished to forget the other." [31]

But absorbing as such links (or *broken* links) of association may be, one would probably look for them in vain in the modern Poes and Conan Doyles, or even Joyces, Wolfes, and Prousts. Which is as it should be: "If there were no distinctions between the fields of psychology and art, the accurate transcript of the therapeutic situation—a psychoanalytic 'case history'—would also be great art. That this cannot be Freud has himself seen clearly." [32] If fiction were to lose sight of this, it would lose the name of art and become merely the metrics of psychopathology.

Notes

1 Notes on the American Muse as Psyche

1. Mary Louise Aswell, ed. *The World Within* (New York, 1947), Introduction, xv.

2. *The Spirit of the Age* (London, 1825), pp. 15–16.

3. Aswell, *The World Within*, xv.

4. "The Very Bent Twig," *The New Yorker*, March 25, 1950, p. 36.

5. *Ibid.*, p. 27.

6. *Saturday Review of Literature*, March 25, 1950, p. 17.

7. *Talks to Teachers on Psychology* (1899) (New York, 1916), pp. 214–15.

8. *Collected Papers on Analytical Psychology*, 2nd ed. (London, 1920), p. 415 (Chap. V: "The Personal and the Impersonal Conscious").

9. *Guy Rivers* (New York, 1834), Vol. 2, p. 314.

10. *Talks to Teachers on Psychology*, p. 82.

11. "Intellectualism—the conception of man as above all a thinking animal, consciously adapting means to rationally chosen ends—fell sick with Rousseau, took to its bed with Kant, and died with Schopenhauer. After two centuries of introspective analysis philosophy found, behind thought, desire; and behind the intellect, instinct." (Will Durant, *The Story of Philosophy*, chap. 7.)

12. Preface to *Germinie Lacerteux* (1864). In Richard Ellmann and Charles Feidelson, Jr., eds. *The Modern Tradition* (New York, 1965), pp. 269–70.

13. *Mimesis* (New York, 1957), p. 437.

14. Emile Zola, *Thérèse Raquin*, trans. Willard R. Trask, 2nd ed. (New York, 1960), Preface, xx.

15. Vladimir Astrov, "Hawthorne and Dostoyevsky as Explorers of the Human Conscience," *New England Quarterly*, XV (June 1942), 300.

16. Susan Glaspell had written the play *Suppressed Desires*, produced in 1917.

17. J. T. Stewart, "Miss Havisham and Miss Grierson," *Furman Studies*, VI (Fall 1958), 21–23.

18. *Freudianism and the Literary Mind*, 2nd ed. (Baton Rouge, 1957), pp. 112–13.

19. Irving Howe, Introduction to *The Bostonians*, The Modern Library (New York, 1956), xxiii–xxiv.

20. "Psychology and Fiction" in *The Doctor Looks at Literature* (New York, 1923), p. 23. "Freud . . . has tremendously influenced almost every modern writer and critic," Stanley Edgar Hyman writes in *The Armed Vision* (1948) (New York, 1955), p. 135.

21. *After the Genteel Tradition* (1937) (Carbondale, 1964), p. 108.

22. *Years of My Youth* (New York, 1916), pp. 187–88.

23. "Wordsworth's poems of this sort . . . are not so much original in kind," writes Robert Mayo, "as they are distinguished by a mature theory of psychology and a serious interest in 'manners and passions.'" Poems about insanity and defective minds were popular in the 1790's. ("The Contemporaneity of the *Lyrical Ballads*," PMLA, LXIX [June 1954], 498–500.)

24. Hyman, *The Armed Vision*, p. 143; Edward Stone, "Melville's Pip and Coleridge's Servant Girl," *American Literature*, XXV (November 1953), 358–60.

25. Robert Humphrey, *Stream of Consciousness in the Modern Novel* (1954) (Berkeley, 1959), p. 118.

26. Harrison Hayford and Merton M. Sealts, Jr., eds. *Billy Budd* (Chicago, 1962), Chap. 21.

27. Hyman, *The Armed Vision*, p. 144.

2   Herman Melville

1. Letter of Herman Melville to Nathaniel Hawthorne, June, 1851.

2. *Ibid.*

3. Clifton Fadiman, Introduction to Heritage Press edition of *Moby-Dick* (1943).

4. Charles Olson, *Call Me Ishmael* (1947) (New York, 1958), pp. 52–58, 68.

5. F. O. Matthiessen, *American Renaissance: Art and Expression in the Age of Emerson and Whitman* (Oxford, 1941), p. 290.

6. As Daniel Hoffman has commented, Ahab becomes "the objectification of those very impulses in his own soul that Ishmael had fled to sea to escape." (*Form and Fable in American Fiction* [1961], New York, 1965, p. 240.)

7. William M. Gibson, "Herman Melville's 'Bartleby the Scrivener' and 'Benito Cereno,'" *The American Renaissance* (Berlin and Bonn, 1962), pp. 107–16.

8. In a mad quip that echoes Hamlet's (IV, iii, 32–34).

3 Henry James

1. F. O. Matthiessen and Kenneth Murdock, eds. *The Notebooks of Henry James* (New York, 1947), pp. 57–58.

2. George M. Baker, *Mose Evans* (New York, 1874), pp. 71–72. All other page references (directly following the passages quoted) are to this edition.

3. "Editor's Literary Record," *Harper's New Monthly Magazine*, LXIX (September 1874), 593.

4. *The Complete Tales of Henry James* (Philadelphia, 1963), V, 11.

5. James's entry in his *Notebooks* about Gosse's information appears again in the Preface to the volume (XV) of the New York Edition in which "The Author of 'Beltraffio'" was reprinted.

6. That Henry James had read *Mose Evans* when he wrote "The Author of 'Beltraffio,'" we have no proof; that he easily could have, there is no doubt. Its author had achieved a reputation in 1866 with his *Inside: A Chronicle of Secession*. When *Mose Evans* appeared in book form, William Dean Howells gave it a long review in the August 1874 issue of *The Atlantic Monthly*. It had appeared there in six installments, during the first six months of 1874. In three of these six numbers Henry James was also appearing. Under these circumstances it seems safe to assume that James read Baker's novel.

That James's own account of the source of "The Author of 'Beltraffio'" makes no allowance for this possibility by no means rules it out. Scholarship has submitted considerable evidence over the years that the *Notebooks* and Prefaces are not the only guide to James's sources, nor even a reliable one.

7. Edmund Wilson, "Philoctetes: The Wound and the Bow," *The Wound and the Bow* (London, 1961), pp. 249, 259, 261.

8. Yet his very offending of "the finer female sense" kept women reading Henry James. By 1902 Howells could write that "to read him if for nothing but to condemn him, is the high intellectual experience of the daughters of mothers whose indignant girlhood resented while it adored his portraits of American women." ("Mr. James's Masterpiece;" *Harper's Bazar*, XXXVI [January 1902], 9.)

4 Stephen Crane

1. "Pity and Fear in 'The Blue Hotel,' " *American Quarterly*, IV (Spring 1952), 75.

2. Robert W. Stallman, "Stephen Crane: A Revaluation," in *Critiques and Essays on Modern Fiction: 1920–1951*, ed. John W. Aldridge, (New York, 1952), p. 253.

James W. Colvert thinks that Crane may have taken lessons in color from Rudyard Kipling. ("The Origins of Stephen Crane's Literary Creed," University of Texas *Studies in English*, XXIV [1955], 179–88.)

3. R. W. Stallman and Lillian Gilkes, eds. *Stephen Crane: Letters* (New York and London, 1960), p. 336.

4. *Stephen Crane* (New York, 1923), p. 113.

5. Specifically, on brown, which excited in Crane's characters a feeling of calmness, of peace. To Henry Fleming, for example, in *The Red Badge of Courage*, in flight into the forest from the violence of battle, "pine needles were a gentle brown carpet."

6. The piece of reporting on the Greco-Turkish war, date-lined Athens, May 11, 1897 (printed in the *New York Journal*, Wednesday, May 12, 1897, p. 3) in which Crane lamented the order to the Greek army to retreat given by the Crown Prince was boldly captioned (though not necessarily by Crane): "THE BLUE BADGE OF COWARDICE."

7. "The Many Suns of *The Red Badge of Courage*," *American Literature*, XXIX (November 1957), 322–26.

8. Whether or not the melodramas that Pete takes Maggie to see (*Maggie*, Chap. 8) are ones that Crane himself went to, we know from his mockery of them that he was amused by the "pale-green snowstorms" against which background the hero usually performed his implausible acts of chivalry.

9. Stanley Greenfield goes even further. He finds the Easterner's lecture of little value even as theory: "What could the Easterner have done by standing up for the Swede that the Swede had not done for himself by whipping Johnnie? If old Scully had not given the Swede whiskey and thus made him belligerent, fear might have led to the same end. The cowboy's puffing did nothing one way or the other—and if he had taken a hand, would the Swede have stayed at the hotel and not gone to his death?" ("The Unmistakable Stephen Crane," PMLA, LXXIII [December 1958], 567.)

10. Charles Neider, ed. *Short Novels of the Masters* (New York, 1948); Introduction, p. 23.

11. Stallman, "Stephen Crane: A Revaluation," p. 258.

5 Robert Frost

1. Lionel Trilling, "A Speech on Robert Frost: A Cultural Episode," in *Robert Frost*, ed. James M. Cox (Englewood Cliffs, 1962), pp. 151–58.

2. Nathaniel Hawthorne, "Buds and Bird Voices," *Mosses From an Old Manse* (Boston, 1884), p. 172.

3. Sigmund Freud, *The Ego and Id* (London, 1927), p. 30.

4. *The Myth of Sisyphus*, trans. Justin O'Brien (New York, 1960), pp. 10–11.

5. Nathaniel Hawthorne, *The Marble Faun* (Boston, 1884), p. 125.

6. Hawthorne, "Buds and Bird Voices," p. 181.

6 William Faulkner

1. "Hawthorne and Faulkner," *College English*, XVII (February 1956), 258.

2. *Psychopathia Sexualis* (Chicago, 1928), p. 100. (Part IV: "General Pathology.") Of course, if one considers this offensive obesity merely as the outward sign of the inner deformity—that is, as an elementary form of symbolism—then with it Faulkner as much establishes his kinship with no more recent a writer than Nathaniel Hawthorne, the creator of the deformed Chillingworth. Moreover, Ray B. West, Jr., who concedes Emily's monstrosity, insists (with Brooks and Warren) on calling her story a tragedy in the Aristotelian sense. *See* "Atmosphere and Theme in 'A Rose for Emily,'" *Perspective*, II (1948–49), 239–45.

3. Compare Allen Tate: "Usher becomes the prototype of the Joycean and Jamesian hero who cannot function in the ordinary world," is "for the first time the hero of modern fiction." ("Three Commentaries: Poe, James, and Joyce," *The Sewanee Review*, LVIII [Winter 1950], 2, 4.) Also: "Poe is the transitional figure in modern literature because he discovered our great subject, the disintegration of the modern personality" (*ibid.*).

4. "The Fury of William Faulkner," *The Western Review*, XI (Autumn 1946), 37. Also: "more is implicit [in "Usher"] if we look ahead, or if we relocate Poe's Gothic terrors within a regional perspective. Much that seems forced, in William Faulkner's work, becomes second nature when we think of him as Poe's inheritor. We think of Caddy and Quentin . . . or of Emily Grierson." (Harry Levin, *The Power of Blackness* [New York, 1958], p. 160.)

5. Ray B. West, Jr., "Atmosphere and Theme in 'A Rose for Emily,'" 244–45; and *The Explicator*, VII, No. 1 (October 1948), Item #8. So, too, William Van O'Connor in *The Tangled Fire of William Faulkner* (Minneapolis, 1954), pp. 68–69 fn. But compare C. W. M. Johnson, *The Explicator*, VI, No. 7 (May 1948), Item #45.

6. Van Wyck Brooks, *New England: Indian Summer* (New York, 1940), pp. 493–94.

7. Review of *North of Boston*, *New Republic* (February 20, 1915), 81–82.

8. George Snell, "The Fury of William Faulkner," *The Western Review*, XI (Autumn 1946), 37.

9. Incest, "as symbolic of ingrown-ness" in *The Sound and the Fury* and *Absalom, Absalom!* In these, and in Hawthorne's *Marble Faun*, "incest is used as a symbol of inward-turning. And Hawthorne and Faulkner have related it to evils that have their origins in a diseased sort of self-centeredness." (William Van O'Connor, "Hawthorne and Faulkner: Some Common Ground," in *The Grotesque: An American Genre and Other Essays*, [Carbondale, 1962], pp. 73–74.)

10. *Psychopathia Sexualis* (New York, 1965), pp. 69, 86, 93.

7 J. D. Salinger

1. Frederick C. Crews, *The Sins of the Fathers: Hawthorne's Psychological Themes* (New York, 1966), p. 265.

8 The Paving Stones of Paris

1. Harry Levin writes of modern French critics that "the more they have been put off by what they can only regard as the irrational elements in American life, the more they have been fascinated by the reflection of those elements in American literature." (*"France-Amérique: The Transatlantic Refraction," Comparative Literature Studies*, I [1964], 88.)

2. *Stream of Consciousness in the Modern Novel* (Berkeley, 1959), p. 7.

3. See the final statement of Hobbes' testimony of two hundred years before in Note 11.

4. Francis Galton, *Inquiries into Human Faculty* (1883), Everyman's Library, pp. 136, 140.

5. *Talks to Teachers on Psychology* (1900) (New York, 1916), pp. 85–86.

6. Chapter 13: "A Pilot's Needs."

7. Leon Edel, *The Modern Psychological Novel* (New York, 1959), p. 32.

8. *See* William James, "The History of Opinion Concerning Association," *The Principles of Psychology*, I, pp.

594–604. For the contribution of Bergson's theories to modern fiction (specifically, to the novels of Dorothy Richardson, Virginia Woolf, and Joyce), see Shiv K. Kumar, *Bergson and the Stream of Consciousness Novel* (New York, 1963).

9. Samuel Taylor Coleridge, *Biographia Literaria* (New York and Boston, 1834), pp. 66, 70–72, 78–79.

10. *Ibid*, p. 79.

11. As, for that matter, it does the much earlier one in Hobbes's *Leviathan:* "In a discourse of our present civil war, what could seem more impertinent than to ask (as one did) what was the value of a Roman penny. Yet the coherence to me was manifest enough. For the thought of the war introduced the thought of the delivering up of Christ; and that again the thought of the thirty pence . . . ; and thence easily followed that malicious question; and all this in a moment of time; for thought is quick."

12. *Principles of Psychology*, I, pp. 551–52, 573–77. Much of this, James footnotes, had appeared ten years earlier; and he popularized it ten years later in *Talks to Teachers on Psychology*.

13. Galton, *Inquiries into Human Faculty*, pp. 134, 144.

14. "Mechanism in Thought and Morals" (1891), *The Complete Works of Oliver Wendell Holmes*, Fireside Edition, VIII, 282.

15. Francis O. Matthiessen, *American Renaissance: Art and Expression in the Age of Emerson and Whitman* (Oxford, 1941). "His awareness of 'the haunted mind' . . . points toward our concern with the subconscious" (p. 630).

16. George Eliot attempted something less in *Adam Bede* only a few years later. "Bodily haste and exertion usually leave our thoughts very much at the mercy of our feelings and imagination," she comments in Chapter Four on the mind of a man working hard alone at night building a coffin; accordingly, "scenes of the sad past, and probably sad future, floating before him, and giving place one to the other in swift succession."

17. Sherwood Anderson, *A Story Teller's Story*, (New York, 1924), pp. 393–94.

18. *Look Homeward, Angel*, Modern Library edition, pp. 74–75.

19. Yet no more reticent, at that, than Freud himself. To report his own dreams, he wrote in the Preface to the first edition of *The Interpretation of Dreams*, would be "to reveal to the public gaze more of the intimacies of my mental life than I liked." Yet, report them, he did—but only after expurgating them; after "taking the edge off some of my indiscretions by omissions and substitutions," much to their detriment and that of his peace of mind.

For the fiction writer, of course, the omissions and substitutions—whether in the association of the waking state or of dreams—result not from modesty but from the requirements of art. *See* Oscar Cargill's commentary on *The Sound and the Fury*, Note 26.

20. Quoted from *English Psychology* by William James in *Principles of Psychology*, I, pp. 597–98. He echoes Ribot with his conclusion that "the laws of association *run* the mind." (*Talks to Teachers on Psychology*, p. 84.)

21. Sigmund Freud, *The Interpretation of Dreams* (New York, 1959), pp. 7–10.

22. Joseph Collins, *The Doctor Looks at Literature* (New York, 1923), p. 17; Frederick J. Hoffman, *Freudianism and the Literary Mind*, 2nd ed. (Baton Rouge, 1957), p. 12.

23. Edel, *The Modern Psychological Novel*, p. 19.

24. " 'Wood' seems, from its linguistic connections, to stand in general for female 'material.' . . . Since 'bed and board' constitute marriage, a latter often takes the place of the former in dreams and the sexual complex of ideas is, so far as may be, transposed on to the eating complex." (Freud, *Interpretation of Dreams*, p. 355.)

25. "The Dream of H. C. Earwicker" (reprinted in *The Wound and the Bow*).

26. Oscar Cargill, *Intellectual America* (New York, 1941), pp. 373, 375. My italics. For closer studies of this aspect of Faulkner's art (particularly of *The Sound of*

Fury and *As I Lay Dying*), see the works cited by Edel, Friedman, and Humphrey.

27. Edel, *The Modern Psychological Novel*, p. 16.

28. *Marginalia*, LVII, *The Works of Edgar Allan Poe* (New York, 1884) V, 226.

29. *Confessions of a Young Man*, Chaps. 1, 8.

30. James, *Principles of Psychology*, Vol. I, pp. 567–68.

31. Sigmund Freud, *Psychopathology of Everyday Life* in A. A. Brill, ed. *The Basic Writings of Sigmund Freud*, Modern Library edition (New York, 1938), pp. 35–37.

32. Hoffman, *Freudianism and the Literary Mind*, p. 131.

Index